Impact English

MIKE GOULD (SERIES EDITOR), KIM RICHARDSON, MARY GREEN & JOHN MANNION

Key Stage 3 – Year 8 • Student Book 1

Contents

① Dracula

Aims

▶ Read an extract from *Dracula*

▶ Learn what a Gothic story is

▶ Learn about Gothic language (R14)

▶ Learn about different connectives of time (S7)

▶ Write in the Gothic style

The following extract is from Bram Stoker's *Dracula*. Jonathan Harker, Quincey Morris and friends are chasing Count Dracula, who will rise from his coffin when the sun sets. Quincey has been wounded. They have rushed up to a cart carrying Dracula's coffin and thrown it to the ground. Jonathan's wife, Mina, is surrounded by a ring of fire – a holy circle – to keep her safe from Dracula. She narrates what happens next.

The waxen image

I saw the Count lying within the box upon the earth… He was deathly pale, just like a waxen image, and the red eyes glared with the horrible vindictive look which I knew too well.

As I looked, the eyes saw the sinking sun, and the look of hate
5 in them turned to triumph.

But, on the instant, came the sweep and flash of Jonathan's great knife. I shrieked as I saw it shear through the throat; whilst at the same moment Mr Morris's bowie knife plunged into the heart.

It was like a miracle; but before our very eyes, and almost in
10 the drawing of a breath, the whole body crumbled into dust and

passed from our sight.

I shall be glad as long as I live that even in that moment of final dissolution, there was in the face a look of peace, such as I never could have imagined might have rested there.

15 The Castle of Dracula now stood out against the red sky, and every stone of its broken battlements was articulated against the light of the setting sun.

The gypsies, taking us as in some way the cause of the extraordinary disappearance of the dead man, turned, without a 20 word, and rode away as if for their lives. Those who were unmounted jumped upon the leiter-wagon and shouted to the horsemen not to desert them. The wolves, which had withdrawn to a safe distance, followed in their wake, leaving us alone.

Mr Morris, who had sunk to the ground, leaned on his elbow, 25 holding his hand pressed to his side; the blood still gushed through his fingers. I flew to him, for the Holy circle did not now keep me back; so did the two doctors. Jonathan knelt behind him and the wounded man laid back his head on his shoulder. With a sigh he took, with a feeble effort, my hand in 30 that of his own which was unstained. He must have seen the anguish of my heart in my face, for he smiled at me and said:-

'I am only too happy to have been of service! Oh, God!' he cried suddenly, struggling up to a sitting posture and pointing to me, 'It was worth this to die! Look! Look!'

35 The sun was now right down upon the mountain top, and the red gleams fell upon my face, so that it was bathed in rosy light.

waxen image small model person made of white wax

vindictive desire for revenge

bowie stout hunting knife

dissolution falling apart, death

battlements parapet at the top of a castle, with squared openings for shooting

articulated in the text it means all the structure is displayed

leiter-wagon leading wagon

feeble weak

anguish worry, distress

posture the way the body is held

Key Reading

Narrative texts

This text is an extract from a **narrative**. Its **purpose** is to tell a story in an entertaining way.

The main features of this text are:

● It has a structure that includes an opening (**introduction**), a problem (**complication**), a dramatic moment when everything comes to a head (**crisis**) and an ending (**resolution**) when things are sorted out. For example, *Dracula* has the following structure:

Introduction: Jonathan Harker, a lawyer, is asked to visit a mysterious Count Dracula who lives in Transylvania.

Complication: While there, Jonathan discovers that the Count is a vampire. Dracula sets sail for England determined to seduce Jonathan's wife-to-be (Mina) and friend (Lucy).

Crisis: Lucy becomes a vampire. Jonathan and his friends must release Lucy's soul, save Mina from Dracula and rid the world of him.

Resolution: Dracula's throat is cut and a knife is plunged into his heart.

● It has **characters**, who the story is about. The reader often hears their words and thoughts.

● There is also a **narrator**, who tells the story in either the first person (I/we) or the third person (he/she/it), for example, '*I* saw the Count lying within the box…' is a first person narrative.

● It uses **powerful words**, so that the language of the narrative is interesting to read or listen to. For example, 'The Castle of Dracula now stood out against the *red sky*…'

1 What is the most **important thing** that happens in the extract?

2 Name three of the **characters**.

3 Is the text told mainly in the **first person** or the **third person**? Give reasons for your answer.

4 Find another example of **powerful description** in paragraph 1.

• •

Purpose

The purpose of a narrative is to entertain the reader. One way to do this is to keep the reader's attention. For example, in paragraph 1 the description of Dracula makes the reader want to find out what he might do.

5 Read paragraphs 2 and 3 (but not paragraph 4). What do you want to find out? **Make a list**.

6 Read the rest of the extract. What **two things** do you most want to find out from the list below?
- What happens to Mina
- What happens to Dracula's body
- Whether Morris dies
- Whether Dracula reappears
- What the gypsies do.

Reading for meaning

The Gothic style

A Gothic tale is a tale of horror.

- **Settings** for Gothic tales are usually dramatic and set in the past. For example, ruined castles, secret places and sweeping landscapes.

- **Characters** express strong feelings and desires. They may have nightmares, see visions or go mad.

- **Events** in the plot are also dramatic – there may be a kidnapping or an imprisonment under the power of some evil presence.

- The **language** used in Gothic writing is usually **sensational** (causing feelings of surprise or horror). This creates an air of fear and mystery, and suits the dramatic plot.

> **sensational** causing feelings of surprise or horror

Example A is from *Dracula* and is written using sensational language.

A 'I am only too happy to have been of service! Oh, God!' he cried suddenly, struggling up to a sitting posture and pointing to me, 'It was worth this to die! Look! Look!'

In example B, the extract has been rewritten in a non-Gothic style:

B 'I am only too happy to have been of some use,' he said. Then attempting to sit up he pointed towards the sunset. 'Look,' he said, 'it was worth it.'

7 Find as many **differences** as you can between A and B. Look at:
- words that have been replaced in B
- words that have been left out or turned around in B
- the punctuation.

8 Read examples C and D below. Which is written in the Gothic style? Work in groups and find **three pieces of evidence** to support your choice.

C
My pulse was beating fast, my heart racing! But the creature – seeming to bear down upon me with its great paws – instead rushed headlong towards the gaping chasm. That perilous pit! There, in one mighty leap, the beast spanned the abyss and in an instant, had vanished! Vanished into the forest!

D
My pulse and heart were racing, as the creature gaining speed had almost caught up with me. But instead of sweeping me up in its great paws it flew past, making for the chasm. In one mighty bound the creature had leapt across and almost as quickly had vanished into the forest.

• •

Focus on: Linking by time

Using paragraphs is an important way to link ideas in a text. In a Gothic narrative, paragraphs are sometimes linked by **connectives**, which show several things happening at the same time. This increases the drama of the narrative.

For example, paragraph 1 starts with a description of Count Dracula in his coffin. Then paragraph 2 begins:

As I looked… — Refers to events happening at the same time as those in paragraph 1

9 **a)** Find an example of this use of **connectives** in paragraph 3.

b) Paragraph 6 contains another example of this use of connectives. It is not quite at the beginning of the paragraph. Can you find it?

10 Time connectives link paragraphs by showing what happens next. Which **time connectives** start these two paragraphs?

A
> After the horses were ready Rudolpho helped her into the waiting carriage. He cracked the whip and they began their long and dangerous journey. While they kept to the main track all was well. But when they turned into the woods…

B
> A moment later she heard a sound she had never heard before. It was like…

Key Writing

11 You are a writer of Gothic tales. Your task is to:

● **Continue the second paragraph** from question 10. What happens next on the journey?

● Add a third paragraph to **end the journey dramatically**. Start this paragraph with a time connective that shows what happens next.

Use some of the **sensational language** below or make up your own. Check the meaning of any words you do not know in a dictionary.

● baying wolves
● strange, murky light
● towering, snow-capped mountains
● narrow, hazardous track

② Mrs Ravoon

Aims

▶ Read the poem *Alternative Endings to an Unwritten Ballad*

▶ Learn about Gothic writing (R14)

▶ Learn about comic poetry, word associations and rhyme (W11)

▶ Build a character

▶ Write a poem

Many vivid images spring to mind when reading this poem by Paul Dehn. As you read it you will realise that each verse has a different setting and is like a different ending for a Gothic poem.

Alternative Endings to an Unwritten Ballad

I stole through the dungeons, while everyone slept,
　　Till I came to the cage where the Monster was kept.
There, locked in the arms of a Giant Baboon,
　　Rigid and smiling, lay…MRS RAVOON!

5　I climbed the clock tower in the first morning sun
　　And 'twas midday at least 'ere my journey was done;
But the clock never sounded the last stroke of noon,
　　For there, from the clapper, swung MRS RAVOON!

I hauled in the line, and I took my first look
10　At the half-eaten horror that hung from the hook.
I had dragged from the depths of the limpid lagoon
　　The luminous body of MRS RAVOON.

I fled in the storm, the lightning and thunder,
And there, as a flash split the darkness asunder,
15 Chewing a rat's-tail and mumbling a rune,
Mad in the moat squatted MRS RAVOON!

I stood by the waters so green and so thick,
And I stirred at the scum with my old, withered stick;
When there rose through the ooze, like a monstrous balloon,
20 The bloated cadaver of MRS RAVOON.

Facing the fens, I looked back from the shore
Where all had been empty a moment before;
And there by the light of the Lincolnshire moon,
Immense on the marshes, stood...MRS RAVOON!

'twas it was
'ere before
ballad a story in verse
clapper the striker or tongue of a bell
limpid clear
luminous bright and shining
asunder (old-fashioned term) apart
rune a mark or letter of magic or mysterious importance
cadaver a corpse
fens marshland

Key Reading

Poetry

This text is a **poem**. Its **purpose** is to explore feelings and ideas.

A poem is made up of **images, rhythm** and **form**.
- The **images** are the pictures made by the words.
- The **rhythm** is like the beat in music.
- The **form** is the framework or pattern of the poem. Poems are written in **lines** not sentences.

Other important features of poetry are:
- Some poems **rhyme**, for example, the words 'slept' and 'kept' rhyme in this poem.
- Some poems are written in **free verse**. They have lines of different lengths with different rhythms. (Some free verse contains rhyme.)

1 **Who** or **what** is the poem about?

2 What kinds of **setting** are mentioned in the poem?

3 The rhythm of the poem is the same in each verse. In other words, the poem has a regular rhythm. Find three other things that are **regular** or **repeated** in the poem.

Purpose

4 What is the **main reason** why this poem was written? Choose from the following options, giving reasons for your choice:
- to frighten the reader
- to make fun of the Gothic style
- to make the reader laugh
- to explain what happened to Mrs Ravoon.

Reading for meaning

Gothic tales of horror and the supernatural are very dramatic, so they are easy to make fun of. This is what the poet does in *Alternative Endings to an Unwritten Ballad*. For example, when you hear the name 'Dracula', you probably think of vampires. However, when you hear the name 'Mrs Ravoon', a picture of a ghost probably does not spring to mind.

5 What **picture** does the name 'Mrs Ravoon' conjure up in your mind? Discuss your ideas with a partner.

The reader never knows who or what Mrs Ravoon really is or where she comes from. But there are clues in the poem that help to build a picture.

6 Identify the **word in the glossary** that gives specific information about Mrs Ravoon.

Read the first verse of the poem again.

> I stole through the dungeons, while everyone slept,
> Till I came to the cage where the Monster was kept.
> There, locked in the arms of a Giant Baboon,
> Rigid and smiling, lay...MRS RAVOON!

These words give more information about Mrs Ravoon

7 a) How does the word '**rigid**' fit with your answer to question 6?

b) Why might Mrs Ravoon be **smiling**?

14

R14

8 a) Use the words you have collected to build up a **picture** of Mrs Ravoon using a **spidergram** like the one below.

smiling ← **Mrs Ravoon** → rigid

b) Check the **last two lines** of the other verses for more words that describe Mrs Ravoon. Add them to your spidergram.

9 **Write three sentences** describing Mrs Ravoon, using the information from your spidergram.

. . . .

Focus on: Rhyming associations

Although the name 'Mrs Ravoon' is funny, it also has associations with death through other rhyming words. For example:

$$Ravoon \rightarrow tomb \rightarrow doom$$

10 a) Add any words that **rhyme** or almost rhyme with 'Ravoon', to make a longer chain. Use a rhyming dictionary if it helps.

b) Do the same with the following words:

● spell   ● flinch

● sore   ● blood.

Keep your rhyming words ready for question 12.

Key Writing

11 Refer back to the spidergram you did for Mrs Ravoon in question 8. Working in groups, **make another spidergram**, this time for a vampire.

a) Brainstorm a **name** for your vampire to do with death or the supernatural. For example:

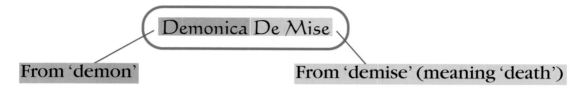

Write the name of your vampire at the centre of your spidergram.

b) Brainstorm ideas about **what your character is like** and add these around your vampire's name on the spidergram.

c) To gather useful vocabulary, look up **key words** in a thesaurus. Start with Gothic words from the poem and then use the following words:

- fang
- sunset
- graveyard
- blood
- coffin
- fright.

Add any words to the spidergram that suit your vampire's character.

12 Working on your own, **write the last verse** of a poem in which you see your vampire. Follow the verse pattern of *Alternative Endings to an Unwritten Ballad*. Your poem could begin:

'Far below in the pit, where the sun never reaches...'

Remember:

- Don't force the rhymes. Choose those that fit the meaning best. Look back at the rhymes you made in question 10, to see if there are any you can use.

- Keep the rhythm of the lines regular.

③ Vlad the Impaler

Aims

- Read discursive writing about Vlad the Impaler
- Identify points 'for' and 'against' an issue
- Identify evidence in the text
- Discuss and present a point of view (S&L10)

Who exactly was Vlad the Impaler and why is he often associated with Dracula? Read the following and find out.

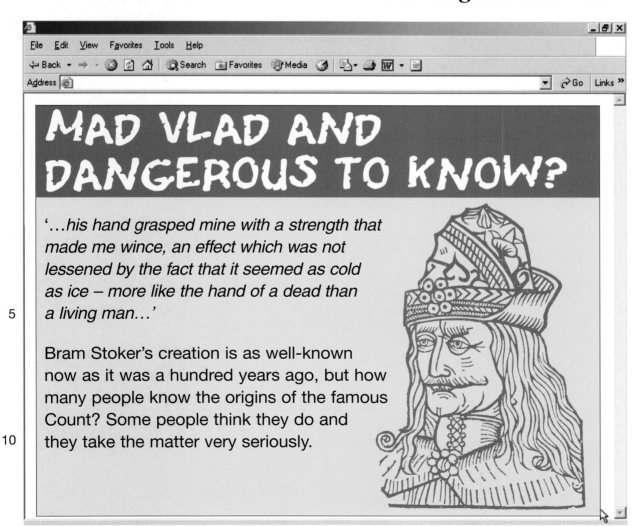

MAD VLAD AND DANGEROUS TO KNOW?

'…his hand grasped mine with a strength that made me wince, an effect which was not lessened by the fact that it seemed as cold as ice – more like the hand of a dead than a living man…'

5

Bram Stoker's creation is as well-known now as it was a hundred years ago, but how many people know the origins of the famous Count? Some people think they do and they take the matter very seriously.

10

Born in 1431, Vlad, the Romanian Prince of Wallachia, was a ruler
of fanatical cruelty. Having seen his father murdered, his brother tortured
and been imprisoned himself, he wreaked havoc on anyone who crossed
his path. Many of his victims were subjected to a painful death. They
15 were flayed alive, boiled in oil, beheaded, burnt, chopped into pieces or
had wooden stakes driven through their bodies. His castle was
surrounded by impaled corpses. Impalement seems to have been his
preferred method of torture and he became known as Vlad the Impaler.

But how far did Bram Stoker base his vampire on Vlad? There is
20 certainly evidence to suggest that he knew of his existence. In 1890,
while on holiday in Whitby, Yorkshire, where much of the novel is set, he
discovered William Wilkinson's book *An Account of the Principalities of
Wallachia and Moldavia* and a reference to a warrior Dracula. It was
from this he chose the name for his novel. Interestingly Vlad went by (or
25 was given) the name 'Dracul'.

Those who are convinced that Vlad is Bram Stoker's character point
to other evidence: that his idea of driving a weapon through his vampire
came from Vlad's liking for impalement. They also claim that the Count
is based on a portrait of Vlad which has the inscription, 'A wonderous
30 and frightening story about a great bloodthirsty berserker called
Dracula'. Some have even suggested that Vlad drank his victim's blood.

However, it is also possible that beyond the reference to Dracula,
Bram Stoker knew little more about Vlad. Elizabeth Miller points out
that nowhere in the novel is Vlad referred to, nor are any of his habits
35 recounted. To draw a connection between driving a stake through a
vampire and impaling victims is too far-fetched, she suggests. As for
the portrait, what proof is there? Bram Stoker may have read countless
descriptions of Gothic characters. Finally, she claims there is no
evidence in any historical data that refers to Vlad as a vampire.

40 So, is Vlad Dracula and
Dracula Vlad? Or is Bram
Stoker's creation the work of a
fertile imagination with a little
help from the Whitby public
library? You can decide.

wince to shrink or give a start back
fanatical excessive
wreak to cause or inflict
havoc chaos, destruction
flay to strip off the skin
impale to pierce with a pointed object
principality the territory or land belonging to a prince
inscription words carved or engraved on something
beserker violent warrior

Key Reading

Discursive texts

This text is a **discursive** text. The **purpose** of discursive writing is to present an argument from different points of view.

The main features of this text are:

- It has a **form** that consists of an **opening statement**, a **series of points on both sides** of the issue supported by **evidence** and a **conclusion**. For example, the article makes the following point supported by evidence: 'the Count is based on a portrait of Vlad which has the inscription, "A wonderous…"'

- It includes **phrases at the start of sentences** that signal which side of the issue is being written about, for example: 'Those who are convinced that Vlad is Bram Stoker's character…'

- It uses **formal language** written mainly in the **present tense**, for example, 'To draw a connection… *is* too far-fetched.'

1 Which paragraph tells the reader **what the text is about**?

2 a) Which paragraph gives a **description** of Vlad?
  b) **Find three facts** about him.

3 Identify **one piece of evidence** from paragraph 4 that supports the view that Vlad inspired Bram Stoker to write *Dracula.*

4 The text is mainly written in the present tense. However, there are times when the **past tense** is used. Find two examples from two different paragraphs.

Purpose

5 A discursive text presents views on a particular issue. What **issue** is being discussed in this article? Is it whether or not:

- Vlad was a vampire
- Bram Stoker's *Dracula* is based on Vlad
- Vlad was worse than Dracula
- such things as vampires exist?

Reading for meaning

Discursive texts can be structured to present arguments in two ways.

A

Some present one point of view followed by the opposite point of view. Then the next point is made, followed by its opposite, and so on.

B

Some discursive accounts will present *all* the points of one argument, and then *all* the points for the opposite argument.

R10   **6** Look again at the whole text. Which **structure**, **A** or **B**, does this discursive text have?

7 You are going to search paragraphs 4 and 5 of the article for:

● the points that claim **Dracula is based on Vlad**

● the **evidence** given to back them up.

Record your answers in a table like the one below.

Begin by looking for the key words and phrases that make each point, then give the evidence for that point. For example, line 20:

'he knew of his existence'
so we could write in the table:
Bram Stoker knew of Vlad's existence

Then we find the evidence in the text to support it.

Is Dracula based on Vlad?	
Points for	**Evidence**
Bram Stoker knew of Vlad's existence	Wikinson's book (mentions a warrior called Dracula)

8 When you have finished the first table, draw up another for the points **against** Dracula being based on Vlad. Search paragraph 6 for the points and the evidence in the same way.

• •

Focus on: Useful phrases and connectives

There are many useful phrases that help to introduce and link the views and points being made in this discursive account. For example, in line 28 it says:

They also claim that the Count is based on a portrait of Vlad…

9 Find another example of this **kind of phrase** in paragraph 5.

21

As you discovered in the 'Reading for Meaning' section on page 20, discursive texts can present opposite views, one after the other.

10 **Complete these pairs of sentences** using the information you recorded in the tables for questions 7 and 8. The first sentence has been done for you, as an example.

> On the one hand, Bram Stoker knew of Vlad and his name 'Dracula'.
> On the other hand…

> One view is that…
> Alternatively…

Key Speaking and Listening

S&L10

11 **a)** Working in groups, **discuss** how far you think Bram Stoker's *Dracula* is based on the life of Vlad the Impaler.

- To help you remember the viewpoints on both sides, refer to the notes you made in the tables for questions 7 and 8.

- You will also need to look carefully at the evidence. For example, we believe we know where Bram Stoker got the *name* 'Dracula' from, but we don't know how far the *character* of Dracula is based on Vlad the Impaler. This evidence will help you weigh up the points for and against.

b) At the end of your discussion, come to a group decision on the issue. Note down the **main reasons** for your group's decision.

c) Choose one member of your group to **report** your decision to another group.

④ Unit 1 Assignment: Gothic storyteller

Assessment Focuses

▶ **AF3** Organise and present whole texts effectively, sequencing and structuring information, ideas and events

> **You:** are a storyteller.
>
> **Your task:** to write a Gothic story or **narrative** for other students to read.

Stage 1

First choose a setting for your story from the following:

- a lonely graveyard
- a derelict theatre
- an abandoned fairground.

Describe the scene:
What time of day/night is it? What can you see and hear?

Use powerful description to give your setting a Gothic feel:
Include adjectives – for example, 'It became a *devilish* shape in the *midnight* air…' and adverbs – for example, 'It crept *stealthily*…'

Now **introduce your main character**. In this story you are the main character so you will need to write in the **first person** and use the **past tense**.

Points to remember:

● Explain to your readers why you are in this setting. Is it by accident or on purpose?

● Do not give too much direct information about yourself. Instead of telling the reader, **show them** through your description. For example, instead of writing 'I was scared', you could write 'I could feel the beads of sweat above my lip.' This *shows* the reader that you are scared, even though you have not said so directly.

Stage 2

● Having created your setting, you now need to introduce the **problem** to overcome.

  Introduce a 'presence' (for example, a ghost, vampire or unknown creature). Does it approach you? Is it in distress? Is it frightening you? Have you met this presence before?

● Then think about the **crisis** of your story.

  What do you do? Do you have a clever way of tricking the evil presence? Do you have any supernatural powers? Do you need to use them or not?

● Finally, what will be the **ending** to your story?

  What happens to you? What happens to the presence? Does your plan to resolve the crisis work? Perhaps you get unexpected help. If so, how? Is it a happy or a sad ending for you?

Stage 3

Use your plan to **write your story**.

Remember to make the story flow better by:

- using connectives to link ideas **within** paragraphs. For example, two things can happen at the same time:

  'As it suddenly leapt forward, I heard the...'

- using connectives to link ideas **across** paragraphs. For example, to shift to another scene you could begin a paragraph with:

  'Meanwhile, at the other side of the...'

Challenge

Look back at the language you used to describe a scene or events in your story. Make it more Gothic in style by adding **dramatic words** or **phrases**.

Tales retold

① The Pig Scrolls

Aims

▶ Read an extract from a novel set in ancient Greece

▶ Experiment with figurative language (Wr6)

▶ Develop an imaginative treatment of a traditional tale (Wr8)

This is an extract from *The Pig Scrolls* by Paul Shipton. It is set in Ancient Greece. Gryllus, who has been turned into a pig, is being taken on a journey by Sibyl, a prophetess. Their way through the mountains is blocked by a gigantic figure carved from the rock, with the body of a lion and the face of a human.

THE PIG AND THE SPHINX

Sibyl was staring at the immense figure grimly. 'Er...Gryllus, I don't think a sculptor made this...' Her voice wobbled. 'I think that's the Sphinx. You know, the real Sphinx.'

'Not possible!' I scoffed. 'The Sphinx guarded the gates to Thebes, donkey's years ago! How could it be here? You're just being para–'

5

The Sphinx's great stone eyes opened. Slate-grey pupils levelled their steady gaze at us. If the cold look in those eyes was anything to go by, it wasn't about to win any Cuddliest Monster competitions. The rest of the stone creature's body didn't even twitch.

'–noid.'

10

Terror grabbed me by the roll of fat at the back of my neck and gave me a good shake. My bristles stood on end like a crack squad of Spartan soldiers on parade.

'Then again, you may have a point,' I said hurriedly, 'in which
15 case, we really ought to be getting out of here.' I turned to go back
the way we had come, but Sibyl blocked my path.
'We *can't* go back,' she said firmly. 'We can get past the Sphinx,
I know we can. All we have to do is answer a riddle.'
She rested a hand on my back. Was she having a bash at a
20 friendly gesture or making sure I didn't do a runner?
'Gryllus, you're good at riddles and stuff, aren't you?'
I could see where this was leading and I didn't like the scenery.
I might not be one of those big-brained, book-stuffed boffins up at
the Academy in Athens, but I have graduated with honours from
25 the University of Life, which is where I learned the golden rule:
Never – and I Mean Never – Volunteer. For ANYTHING.
'Not a chance!' I said.
Sibyl folded her arms crossly. 'But Gryllus, you told us you were
brilliant at riddles! You said you'd got a million of them!'
30 True, I had heard a great many riddles during the long years of
the Trojan War. I knew all the classics: 'How many Spartans does it
take to screw in a torch-holder?' 'Why did the Hydra cross the
road?' 'What time is it when Pluto, Lord of the Underworld, sits on
your fence?' I probably did know a million of them.
35 'But what if today's question is number one million and one?'
I whined. 'Like I said, NO CHANCE!'
There was a terrible sound like rock grinding and crumbling. In
fact, it *was* rock grinding and crumbling as the Sphinx turned its
tree-trunk sized neck to get a better look at us.
40 'I am the Questioner,' said the Sphinx, its voice stone on stone.
'Who shall be the Answerer?'
And without another word Sibyl took a step forwards.
At that moment, despite the many differences we'd had along the
journey, despite all the squabbles and bickering, I couldn't help
45 truly admiring the bravery of that simple act.
'He is,' said the prophetess, pointing at me.

Sphinx monster in the hills around the city of Thebes who killed
   those who could not answer her riddles
scoffed laughed scornfully
paranoid unnecessarily fearful
Spartan people from Sparta known for their military discipline
graduated with honours gained a good degree
Hydra a snake-like monster with many heads, killed by Heracles
prophetess a woman whose words are inspired by the gods

Key Reading

Narrative texts

This text is a **narrative**. Its **purpose** is to tell a story in an entertaining way.

The main features of this text are:

- It has a **structure** that includes an opening (**introduction**), a problem (**complication**), a dramatic moment when everything comes to a head (**crisis**) and an ending (**resolution**) when things are sorted out. For example, the crisis occurs when Sibyl names Gryllus as the Answerer.

- It has **characters** who the story is about. We often hear their words and thoughts.

- It has a **narrator** who tells the story in either the first person (I/we) or the third person (he/she/it). In this text the narrator is one of the characters and tells the story in the first person, for example, '*I* could see where this was leading'.

- It uses **expressive** and **descriptive language**, for example, '"Not possible!" I scoffed.'

- The characters' words are quoted using **direct speech**, for example, '"I am the Questioner," *said* the Sphinx.' ('Said is the reporting verb')

1 Who are the **three characters** in this extract?

2 What is **unusual** about each of the characters?

3 What is the **main problem** the characters face in this episode?

4 At which point in the extract does the author remind the reader that the **narrator is a pig**?

5 'Slate-grey pupils levelled their steady gaze at us' (lines 6–7). What **effect** does the author want to create with this description?

6 **Who** is speaking in line 10? How do you know?

• •

Purpose

7 What do you think is the author's **main purpose** in writing this extract. Is it:

  ● to retell the myth of the Sphinx for modern readers
  ● to make his readers laugh
  ● to poke fun at a Greek myth
  ● to move the plot of the book forward?

Point to evidence in the text to support your answer.

• •

Reading for meaning

8 **a)** At what point exactly does Gryllus realise that he is looking at the Sphinx?

  b) How does the author make the Sphinx a frightening creature?

9 **a)** What **word class** do the underlined words belong to?
  'Sibyl was staring at the immense figure _grimly_.'
  '"We can't go back," she said _firmly_.'

  b) What do words like this add to the dialogue? What more do we learn about the **character's words or feelings**?

One technique that the author uses for comic effect is a sudden change in tone or mood, for example:

'You're just being para–'

The Sphinx's great stone eyes opened...

'–noid.'

Gryllus is confident that this isn't the Sphinx

You can imagine Gryllus's face falling as he ends the word 'paranoid'

10 **Analyse** the **final seven lines** of the extract in the same way. How does the author build up one mood then suddenly change it?

11 This version of a Greek myth includes references to modern life. For example, 'to win any Cuddliest Monster competitions...'

Identify another **reference to modern life** and explain why the author has included it.

12 A Greek myth is usually narrated in serious, formal language. This version uses a lot of informal language, for example, *'donkey's years ago'*.

a) Find three more examples of **informal language**.

b) What is the overall **effect** of this language?

· ·

Focus on: Similes

This extract is not just a series of jokes. The author also tries to make you imagine the scene through his use of language.

One type of imagery the author uses is called a **simile**. A simile is a statement that compares one thing to another, using the words 'like' or 'as'. Look at this example from the extract:

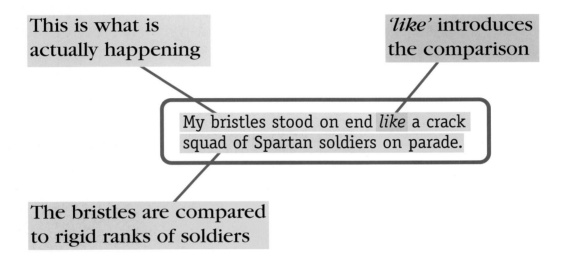

This is what is actually happening

'*like*' introduces the comparison

My bristles stood on end *like* a crack squad of Spartan soldiers on parade.

The bristles are compared to rigid ranks of soldiers

13 How does this simile help you to **picture the scene** in a particular way?

14 In pairs, **complete the similes** below. The images you use should make the reader see each scene in a special way. The first one has been done for you.

Wr6

a) The gymnast leapt through the air like a *shooting star.*

b) Dark clouds gathered overhead like…

c) Her teeth chattered with cold as…

d) He polished his motorbike as…

Key Writing

15 Imagine that you are continuing the story of Gryllus and Sibyl. To make the riddle scene funny, try to make it sound like a **TV game show** in which Gryllus is a contestant and the Sphinx is the quizmaster. In the original story, the riddle was: 'What creature walks on four legs in the morning, two in the afternoon and three in the evening?'

a) Here are some of the **features of a game show** that you could refer to. Discuss these features with a partner. How could you use one or two of them?

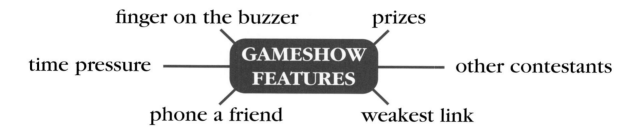

b) Now **role-play** a dialogue with your partner. One of you will play Gryllus, the other will play the Sphinx. Think about these issues:

● Will you use the original riddle or change it?

● Will you bring Sibyl in somehow, perhaps as another contestant?

After your role play, jot down ideas for your narrative.

c) Now **draft your episode** together. You may want to begin like this:

'Here is your riddle, Answerer,' roared the Sphinx.
'Can't I have a starter for ten first?' I whimpered.

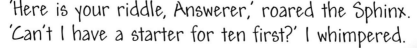

② Urban legends

Aims

◗ Read an explanation text about urban legends

◗ Remind yourself of the key features of explanation texts

◗ Explore how sentences are grouped together in paragraphs (S6)

◗ Write a short explanation (Wr11)

The following text is adapted from the 'How Stuff Works' website.

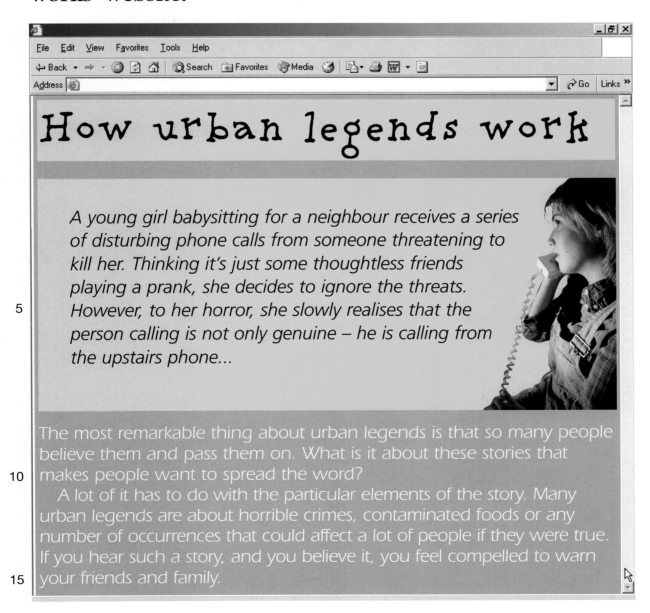

How urban legends work

A young girl babysitting for a neighbour receives a series of disturbing phone calls from someone threatening to kill her. Thinking it's just some thoughtless friends playing a prank, she decides to ignore the threats.
5 *However, to her horror, she slowly realises that the person calling is not only genuine – he is calling from the upstairs phone...*

The most remarkable thing about urban legends is that so many people believe them and pass them on. What is it about these stories that
10 makes people want to spread the word?

A lot of it has to do with the particular elements of the story. Many urban legends are about horrible crimes, contaminated foods or any number of occurrences that could affect a lot of people if they were true. If you hear such a story, and you believe it, you feel compelled to warn
15 your friends and family.

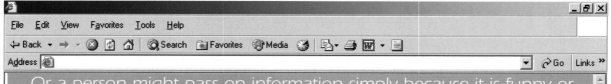

Or a person might pass on information simply because it is funny or interesting. When you first hear the story, you are amazed that such a thing has occurred. When told correctly, a good urban legend will have you on the edge of your seat. It's human nature to want to spread this
20 feeling to others, and be the one who's got everyone waiting to hear how the story turns out. Even if you hear it as a made-up joke, you might be tempted to personalise the tale by claiming it happened to a friend. Basically, people love to tell a good story.

Many people believe an urban legend must be true because it is
25 reported by a newspaper, or other 'authoritative source'. The large number of Halloween stories (razors in apples, needles in candy) is an example of this. There are no documented cases of contamination of Halloween candy, but the media and police issue warnings year after year. Journalists, police officers and other authorities do get things
30 wrong from time to time.

Another reason such stories get passed on is because the details make them seem real. You may have heard stories of children being kidnapped from a specific location, such as a local department store, or you may have heard about various gang initiations that occurred in a
35 specific part of your town. Since you are familiar with the setting – you know it's a real place – the story sounds real. This level of detail also plays into your own fears and anxieties about what could happen to you in the places you visit regularly.

---

contaminated infected
compelled forced
personalise make it refer to someone you know
authoritative reliable, official
documented recorded
initiation a ceremony that marks someone's entry into a club

Key Reading

Explanation texts

This is an **explanation** text. Its **purpose** is to help the reader understand how something works or why something has happened.

The main features of this text are:

● It has a series of **clear and logical steps**, for example, the first paragraph of the main text (lines 8–10) makes it clear exactly what this text is setting out to explain.

● It uses **causal language**, which shows how one thing causes another. For example, '*If* you hear such a story, *and* you believe it, you feel compelled to warn your friends.'

● It uses **formal and impersonal language**, for example, 'There are no documented cases of contamination of Halloween candy.'

1 What is the **first reason** given in the article to explain how urban legends work?

2 The following sentence uses causal language:

> Or a person might pass on information simply because it is funny or interesting.

Identify what is **causing** what to happen.

3 Which words or phrases make the following sentence **formal**?

> You might be tempted to personalise the tale.

Purpose

4 What is the **main purpose** of this text? Is it:

- to explain what makes urban legends so gripping
- to describe the different kinds of urban legends
- to explain what makes people want to pass on urban legends?

5 a) Which part of this text is **not an explanation**?

b) Why do you think it has been included here?

Reading for meaning

6 The main part of the article begins with a question (lines 9–10). An explanation text is supposed to give answers, not ask questions. What do you think the **role of this question** is?

The writer gives four reasons why so many people believe in urban legends. These are:

- Urban legends are often **reported as true** in newspapers and elsewhere.
- The stories contain things you want to **warn** your family and friends about.
- The stories seem real because of the **local detail**.
- The stories are so **funny** or **amazing** that you want them to be true.

7 Find the place where each of these reasons is discussed in the text.

8 a) Identify two verbs in the **present tense** in paragraph 2 (lines 11–15).

b) Why is the present tense usually used in explanation texts?

9 The writer uses causal connectives to highlight the link between cause and effect. For example, 'Another reason such stories get passed on is *because* the details make them seem real.'

a) Write down three examples of **causal language** in paragraph 3.

b) Underline the **causal connective** in each case.

Grammar for reading

A **connective** is a word or phrase that shows the connection between clauses or sentences. **Causal connectives** include 'because', 'if', 'when' and 'since', for example: 'When you turn the key in the lock, the door will open.'

Focus on: Grouping sentences into paragraphs

This explanation text uses paragraphs to separate out each reason why people believe in urban legends. You are now going to look at paragraphing in more detail.

Sentences can be grouped into paragraphs in different ways. Look at the examples of paragraph openings below and on page 38:

Paragraph focus (or main point)

Turning the handle clockwise will lock the door. If you hear a double click, this means...

The rest of the paragraph **expands on the main point**

Paragraph focus (or main point)

> Every member of the team contributed to the victory. Beckham, for example...

The rest of the paragraph **gives examples**

Paragraph focus (or main point)

> The process is simple. First you phone 0118 345345. Then you...

The rest of the paragraph **gives a list in time order**

10 In pairs, analyse the five paragraphs of *How urban legends work*. **Complete a table** like the one below for each paragraph.

S6

Paragraph number	Paragraph focus	Purpose of paragraph	Role of sentences in rest of paragraph
1	The most remarkable thing about urban legends...	To introduce the text	A question to make the topic really clear
2	A lot of it has to do with the particular elements of the story...		

Key Writing

 Wr11 **11** Your task is to **write an explanation** of why urban legends are so popular.

 a) Brainstorm ideas to add to those in the spidergram below, together with a partner:

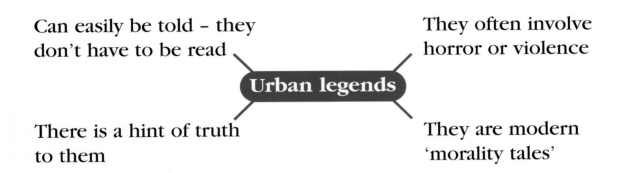

Can easily be told – they don't have to be read

They often involve horror or violence

Urban legends

There is a hint of truth to them

They are modern 'morality tales'

b) Now choose one of the reasons you have identified to write a paragraph about.

- Begin with the **paragraph focus**. This tells the reader the purpose of the paragraph.

- **Group the rest of the sentences together** in a logical way. They must relate to the paragraph focus.

- Use some **causal connectives** in your explanation.

Your **paragraph** could begin like this:

- One reason urban legends are so popular is...
- It is always fascinating when...
- People love to tell stories...

Casual connectives that you could use:

- because
- since
- when
- as a result.
- if

The growth of a legend

Aims

❯ Read a magazine article about Robin Hood
❯ Remind yourself about the key features of analysis texts
❯ Examine the main uses of the comma (S3)
❯ Prepare a courtroom speech (S&L2)

The following text is adapted from a magazine article.

Analysis - Living Legends

Robin Hood: Prince of Thieves or Just a Petty Thief?

Robin Hood – we all know him, don't we? That heroic figure dressed in camouflage green, racing through Sherwood Forest with the gorgeous Marian by his side, stealing from the greedy, cowardly rich to give to the poor. He
5 was the victim of a terrible injustice meted out by the evil Sheriff of Nottingham, and became an outlaw. But he was loved by ordinary people, as he only used violence against the 'baddies'
10 and only killed in self-defence.

This is the story that we've all grown up with. But the legend of Robin Hood wasn't always like this. What makes legends so endlessly fascinating is that they adapt to the times: people
15 come to have different interests and different beliefs, and the way they tell their favourite stories reflects these changes. So legends have a habit of changing as the years pass.

> *His deeds are sung all over England… he was the prince of robbers, and the most humane. He permitted no harm to women, nor seized the goods of the poor, but helped them generously with what he took from abbots.*
>
> *From a history of Britain, 1521*

*He took Sir Guy's head by the hair,
And stuck it on the end of his bow:
'You have been a traitor all your life,
To which there must come an end.'*

*Robin pulled out an Irish knife,
And slashed Sir Guy in the face,
So that no one of a woman born
Could tell who Sir Guy was.*

From a 15th century poem

20 Let's turn back the clock to the Middle Ages. In the original legend of Robin Hood – or at least all that we can glean from the poems and a fragment of a play that have survived – Robin helps a knight with a debt, then recovers the money by robbing the abbot who imposed the debt. In one poem Robin disguises himself as a potter and captures and kills the sheriff; in another, he kills Guy of Gisborne, a medieval

25 'bounty hunter' who is after him, savagely maltreating the corpse. In another, Robin himself is killed through the treachery of a cousin.

This hardly fits with the picture of the greenwood hero painted at the start! Robin is little more than a bold robber. He is also a small landowner, not a peasant or a knight – and certainly not a nobleman.

30 He lives in the forest of Barnsdale in York, not Sherwood Forest in Nottingham, and there is no Maid Marian.

Over the centuries, the legend lost some of these features and gathered others. The Friar and Maid Marian, for example, were originally characters in the Morris dances. At some point around

35 1500 they entered the Robin Hood story, as Robin became celebrated as part of the spring festival. Later on he became a nobleman, the Earl of Huntingdon; later still he turned into the swashbuckling romantic hero that we see in the early films.

No doubt in the 22nd century the legend of Robin Hood will speak to
40 us differently still.

meted out carried out
humane kind, civilised
glean pick up
bounty hunter someone paid money to capture or kill outlaws

maltreating treating badly
greenwood a leafy or woody forest
swashbuckling adventurous, daredevil swordsman

41

Key Reading

Analysis texts

This text is an **analysis**. Its **purpose** is to analyse or explore a topic in detail.

The main features of this text are:

● It **states the issue** at the start then **explores** it by making points carefully. For example, the second paragraph makes the main point.

● It uses **evidence** to support the points being made, for example, the quotes in the margin are evidence.

● It uses **connectives** of contrast, cause and effect, and of time. For example, '…and became an outlaw. *But* he was loved by the ordinary people (contrast)'; '*Later on* he became a nobleman (time).'

1 From the title, what **aspect** of Robin Hood is being analysed?

2 Paragraph 2 spells out the **main point** of this text. **Summarise** this point in one sentence.

3 The first quotation in the margin supports the traditional view of Robin Hood, as told in paragraph 1. Why has the **second quotation** been included?

4 'So legends have a habit of changing as the years pass' (lines 17–18).

    a) How does this sentence **link** to the ones before it?

    b) Which **connective** in the sentence makes this clear?

Purpose

5 What is the **main purpose** of this text? Is it:
- to tell the story of Robin Hood
- to explore how and why the legend of Robin Hood has changed
- to argue that Robin Hood was just a petty thief
- to describe what the historical sources say about Robin Hood?

Point to the evidence in the text that supports your answer.

Reading for meaning

6 According to this text, the original legend of Robin Hood was different to the legend we know today. Find some of these **differences** in paragraphs 3 and 4. Then record them in a table, like the one below.

Original legend	Legend as known today
Robin lives in Barnsdale, York	He lives in Sherwood Forest, Nottingham

7 According to the original legend, what **kind of person** was Robin Hood? Give reasons for your answer.

8 Look at the **first-person references** in these sentences. What effect do they have on the reader?

- *'This is the story that we've all grown up with'* (line 11)
- *'Let's turn back the clock to the Middle Ages'* (line 19)

9 What does the writer mean by his last sentence: 'No doubt in the 22nd century the legend of Robin Hood will speak to us differently still'? (lines 39–40)

• •

Focus on: The comma

The comma is a very common punctuation mark. However, it is also commonly misused! Here are some of the main uses of the comma.

To separate words or phrases in a list. For example:

- '… stealing from the greedy, cowardly rich to give to the poor…'
- 'Robin Hood stole from the rich, helped the needy and fought injustice.'

Note that a comma is not needed after 'needy'. A comma is not needed before 'and' in a list.

To separate clauses in a sentence. For example:

- 'But he was loved by ordinary people, as he only used violence…'
- 'Robin helps a knight with a debt, then recovers the money…'

To mark off phrases in the middle of a sentence that give extra detail about something that has already been mentioned. For example:

● 'Guy of Gisbourne, a medieval 'bounty hunter', is savagely killed.'

● 'Robin, a small landowner, lives in the forest of Barnsdale.'

Note that if you use the commas as 'hooks' to take the phrase out of the sentence, the sentence still makes sense.

S3 **10** Using the information above, write out these sentences and **put in the missing commas**.

   a) Robin's closest companions were Little John Maid Marian Alan a Dale and Will Scarlet.

   b) Drawing an arrow from his quiver Robin took aim and fired.

   c) Little John a giant of a man crushed the knight with one blow.

Key Speaking and Listening

11 Robin Hood is in court. The charge against him is that he is no more than a common thief. Working in pairs, it is your job to defend him and prove that Robin is the people's hero.

a) First, **discuss the facts** that are going to support your case. Make brief notes on the following:

● Robin's main aims as an outlaw

● how he treated people

● who supported him and who opposed him

● his personal qualities and background.

For each point, be prepared to back up your judgement with evidence, drawing on points made in the article on pages 40–41 or your own knowledge of the Robin Hood legend.

b) Next, **prepare your speech** for court. Use your notes as your main points and include the following features of analysis:

● a piece of evidence to back up each point

● connectives to show the links between your ideas.

c) Decide who will deliver the speech and who will be on hand to provide or read out the evidence. Practise delivering the speech and make changes to improve it. Be ready to deliver it to the court.

Unit 2 Assignment: The detective

 ## Assessment Focus

▶ **AF3** Organise and present whole texts effectively, sequencing and structuring information, ideas and events

---

> **You:** are Shylock Holmes, a literary detective.
>
> **Your task:** to analyse two story openings. You must prove which is an urban legend and which is a straight story. You will need your skills in writing an analysis.

Stage 1

Read the two story openings carefully. Then read the 'feature' panels on page 48. Discuss with a partner which opening is from the urban legend and which is from the straight story. Can you identify all the characteristic features of each type of story?

A It was the same most evenings. Sam picked up Becky and drove his wreck to the parking area two miles outside town. There they could play the car radio full blast; they could hang out on their own.

It was already half dark when they heard the local news:

'...escaped from Locksley Prison...convicted for murder...'

Sam stopped drumming his fingers on the tacky steering-wheel.

'... a full-scale hunt is under way,' droned the voice on the dashboard. 'Police are advising members of the public not to approach him. He is extremely dangerous, and has a hook instead of a right arm.'

'A hook!' said Becky. 'That's horrible.'

'Horrible, horrible!' said Sam, grinning in the dark.

'What was that?' cried Becky, and she jammed herself against Sam...

B Did you hear what happened to this couple? They're friends of someone Jack knows. They're on a date, and they've driven out to a quiet country road. They hear this report on the local radio about an escaped killer with a hooked hand, and the girl's getting really nervous. He was supposed to use it on all his victims – the hook, I mean. Anyway, the girl gets so scared, and thinks she's hearing things, like a tapping on the outside of the door…

Features of a straight story:
- Characters who you can become interested in
- Direct speech, in quote marks
- Imaginative use of language
- Narrative with lots of detail.

Features of an urban legend:
- 'Cardboard' characters
- Mostly narrative, little direct speech
- Plain language, reflecting speech
- Simple narrative, including only basic facts.

Stage 2

On your own, jot down at least six points that help to prove your theory. Write them in **note form**, and put the **evidence** next to them. For example:

note

Characters are named (in story A) – as in straight stories.

'Sam picked up Becky'

evidence

Stage 3

Now **plan your report**. Organise your notes into three paragraphs:

- **Paragraph 1:** state clearly the question to be answered
- **Paragraph 2:** show what kind of text passage **A** is
- **Paragraph 3:** show what kind of text passage **B** is.

Stage 4

Now **write your report**. Remember to:

- begin each paragraph with a sentence stating the **main point**
- use **evidence** to back up your points
- use **connectives** (for example, 'because', 'however', 'but') to make the links between your ideas clear.

Challenge

Add a **conclusion** to your report. This would summarise your findings, perhaps by referring back to the introduction.

Unit 3 Magic and illusion

① The Lord of the Rings

Aims

❱ Read an extract from *The Lord of the Rings*

❱ Learn the difference between literal and inferred meaning (R7)

❱ Learn what symbols mean in a narrative (W11)

❱ Create your own symbol

In this extract from early in *The Lord of the Rings* by J.R.R. Tolkien, the wizard Gandalf has paid Frodo an important visit. Something spectacular is about to happen...

An ancient secret

'Give me the ring for a moment.'
  Frodo took it from his breeches-pocket, where it was clasped to a chain that hung from his belt. He unfastened it and handed it slowly to the wizard. It felt suddenly very heavy, as if either it or Frodo himself was in some way reluctant for Gandalf to touch it.

5   Gandalf held it up. It looked to be made of pure and solid gold.
'Can you see any markings on it?' he asked.
  'No,' said Frodo. 'There are none. It is quite plain, and it never shows a scratch or sign of wear.'
  'Well then, look!' To Frodo's astonishment and distress the

10 wizard threw it suddenly into the middle of a glowing corner of the fire. Frodo gave a cry and groped for the tongs; but Gandalf held him back.

15 'Wait!' he said in a commanding voice, giving Frodo a quick look from under his bristling brows.

No apparent change came over the ring. After a while Gandalf got up, closed the shutters outside the window, and drew the curtains. The room became dark and silent, though the clack of Sam's shears, now nearer to the windows, could still be heard

20 faintly from the garden. For a moment the wizard stood looking at the fire, then he stooped and removed the ring to the hearth with the tongs, and at once picked it up. Frodo gasped.

'It is quite cool,' said Gandalf, 'Take it!' Frodo received it on his shrinking palm: it seemed to have become thicker and heavier

25 than ever.

'Hold it up!' said Gandalf, 'And look closely!'

As Frodo did so, he now saw fine lines, finer than the finest pen-strokes, running along the ring, outside and inside: lines of fire that seemed to form the letters of a flowing script. They shone

30 piercingly bright, and yet remote, as if out of a great depth.

'I cannot read the fiery letters,' said Frodo in a quavering voice.

'No,' said Gandalf, 'but I can. The letters are Elvish, of an ancient mode, but the language is that of Mordor, which I will not utter here. But this in the Common Tongue is what is said,

35 close enough:

One Ring to rule them all, One Ring to find them,
One Ring to bring them all and in the darkness bind them.'

breeches trousers
reluctant unwilling
shears large garden scissors
hearth fireside
tongs tool used for lifting coals from the fire
mode style
utter speak

Key Reading

Narrative texts

This text is an extract from a **narrative**. Its **purpose** is to tell a story in an entertaining way.

The main features of this text are:

- It has a **structure** that includes an opening (**introduction**), a problem (**complication**), a dramatic moment when everything comes to a head (**crisis**) and an ending (**resolution**) when things are sorted out. *The Lord of the Rings* is an **epic narrative**. There are brave deeds and adventures and many complications and crises before the long story comes to an end.

- It has **characters** who the story is about. We often hear their words and thoughts. In an epic narrative the main character is often an ordinary person who is called upon to carry out a special task. Since *The Lord of the Rings* is a fantasy, not all the characters are human. However, we still hear their words and thoughts. For example, ' *"Wait!" he said in a commanding voice…'*

- It has a **narrator**, who usually tells an epic story in the third person (he/she/it). For example, '*then he stooped and removed the ring…'*

- It uses **powerful words**, so that the narrative is interesting to read or listen to, for example, '*They shone piercingly bright, and yet remote…'*

1 What is the **most important thing** that happens in the extract?

2 Who is the **wise character** in the extract? How can you tell?

3 Find another example in paragraph 1 that shows this is a **third-person** narrative.

4 Find a **powerful phrase** that describes the room where Gandalf and Frodo meet.

Purpose

The purpose of a narrative is to entertain the reader. Sometimes the writer does this by making the reader curious.

5 By the end of this extract, what more do you want to know about:

- the ring
- Frodo
- Gandalf?

Reading for meaning

A text can be read in different ways to get different information. **Literal meaning** is information that the reader can be certain of. **Inferred meaning** is information that is hidden so that the reader has to work out or infer what is meant.

The Lord of the Rings contains both kinds of meaning. For example, the following information is literal. It has no hidden meanings.

> 'Give me the ring for a moment.'
> Frodo took it from his breeches-pocket...

However, in lines 4–5 the ring is described in the following way:

> It felt suddenly very heavy, as if either it or Frodo himself was in some way reluctant for Gandalf to touch it.

This suggests the ring 'thinks' or has feelings. So you infer that the ring has some kind of power

6 a) Read the passage below, paying particular attention to the numbered parts.

1

3

> No apparent change came over the ring. After a while *Gandalf got up*, closed the shutters outside the window, and *drew the curtains. The room became dark and silent*, though the clack of Sam's shears, now nearer to the windows, could still be heard faintly from the garden. For a moment the wizard stood looking at the fire, then he stooped and *removed the ring to the hearth with the tongs*, and at once picked it up. *Frodo gasped.*

2

4

5

R7

b) Decide which numbered parts have **literal meanings** and which have **inferred meanings**.

c) Complete a chart for the five numbered parts. Tick the second or third column to show whether the meaning is literal or inferred. If the meaning is inferred, write down its hidden meaning.

Number	Literal meaning	Inferred meaning	Hidden meaning
1	✔		
2			
3			
4			
5			

Focus on: Reading the signs

At a simple level, a **sign** or **symbol** is a picture or expression that means something else. For example, an arrow shows which direction to follow.

Symbols are also found in narratives. In *The Lord of the Rings* the ring is a symbol. However, its meaning is harder to work out. It has more than one meaning, but the reader may not discover all of these until the end of the story. However, you can pick up some clues from this text. For example, on page 54 it was inferred that the ring had some kind of power. This meaning is recorded in the table on page 56.

The ring as a symbol	
Information in extract	**Meaning that can be inferred**
Very heavy, as if reluctant for Gandalf to touch it.	The ring seems to think or feel; has some kind of power.
Pure solid gold.	
No obvious markings on it.	
Cool when heated by fire.	
Becomes heavier when heated.	
Ancient language written in fire revealed.	

W11

7 a) The table above lists further information from the extract about the ring. Discuss what you infer from each piece of information and **make notes** in the second column of the table.

b) Sum up the **main thing** the ring could symbolise from the information you have collected in the table.

Key Writing

8 **a)** You are going to **create your own symbol**. You could start with one of the ideas in the table below.

Symbol	Features	Hidden meaning
Key	Can lock and unlock doors	Imprisonment
Book	Can speak	Knowledge
Crown	Can glow in the dark	Protection

b) Your symbol will have a number of **features**. List them in a similar table. To decide what these features are, ask yourself the following questions:

- What is it made of?
- What can it do?
- What are its weaknesses?
- What are its strengths?

 c) Choose the most important hidden meaning for your symbol and **explain it to a partner**.

② The Nose

> Read the poem *The Nose*
> Learn about the style and form of the poem (R10)
> Identify different kinds of images in the poem
> Write your own poem (Wr7)

This poem by Ian Crichton-Smith tells a strange tale.

The Nose
(after Gogol)

The nose went away by itself
in the early morning
while its owner was asleep.
It walked along the road
5 sniffing at everything.

It thought: I have a personality of my own.
Why should I be attached to a body?
I haven't been allowed to flower.
So much of me has been wasted.

10 And it felt wholly free.
It almost began to dance
The world was so full of scents
it had had no time to notice,

15 when it was attached to a face
    weeping, being blown,
    catching all sorts of germs
    and changing colour.

    But now it was quite at ease
    bowling merrily along
20 like a hoop or a wheel,
    a factory packed with scent.

    And all would have been well
    but that, round about evening,
    having no eyes for guides,
25 it staggered into the path
    of a mouth, and it was gobbled
    rapidly like a sausage
    and chewed by great sour teeth –
    and that was how it died.

Gogol (Nikolai) (1809–1852) a
Russian writer. He wrote a
story called *The Nose*, in
which a man loses his nose

Key Reading

Poetry

This text is a **poem**. Its **purpose** is to explore feelings and ideas.

A poem is made up of **images**, **rhythm** and **form**.

- The **images** are the pictures made by the words.
- The **rhythm** is like the beat in music.
- The **form** is the framework or pattern of the poem. Poems are written in **lines** not sentences.

Other important features of poems are:

- Some poems **rhyme** (for example, the words 'dream' and 'seem' rhyme).
- Some poems are **free verse**. They have lines of different lengths with different rhythms. (Some free verse contains rhyme.)

1 How does the nose **feel** about its face?

2 **What happens** to the nose at the end of the poem?

3 How would you **describe** this poem? You can choose more than one answer.

- It is a poem that tells a story.
- It is a free verse poem.
- It is a poem with a regular beat or rhythm.

4 Can you find any **rhymes** in the poem?

Purpose

5 What do you think is the **main reason** why this poem was written? Choose from the following options, giving reasons for your choice:

- to tell a story
- to make the reader laugh
- to make the reader sad or thoughtful
- to make the writer laugh.

Reading for meaning

The poem tells a simple fantasy-style story. Like most fantasies it is similar to a traditional folk tale. It could almost begin, 'Once upon a time there was a nose...'. However, it also has differences.

6 a) Read this list of features often found in folk tales.

Features of the folk tale:
- strange characters or creatures
- strange events
- a journey.

The main character:
- seeks adventure
- may escape by magic
- may be freed from a spell
- meets danger
- outwits enemies
- triumphs in the end.

b) Now **draw up a chart** like the one on the next page. In column 1 write down those features that *The Nose* **shares** with a folk tale.

c) In column 2 write down those features that *The Nose* **does not share** with a folk tale.

The Nose	
Features shared with a folk tale	**Features not shared with a folk tale**

d) In your view, what is the **most important way** in which *The Nose* **differs** from a folk tale?

• •

Focus on: Building images

Although the poem is told like a simple folk tale, it contains unusual images. Most appeal to the sense of sight. For example, the poem opens with:

> The nose went away by itself
> in the early morning
> while its owner was asleep.

7 a) The image that follows in the first verse (lines 4–5) appeals to a different **sense**. What is it?

b) Why would you expect this poem to contain images that appeal to this particular sense?

c) **Find another example** of an image appealing to this sense in verse 3.

Grammar for reading

A **simile** compares one thing with another using 'like' or 'as'.
A **metaphor** describes one thing as *being* another, using words that are usually associated with the other thing.
Both similes and metaphors are used to develop an image, to make it more vivid.

8 a) Identify the two **similes** in the poem. Write them down using quotation marks.

   b) Then note which **verse** the similes are in.

9 a) Reread verse 6, where the mouth appears. Then **make a spidergram** of the mouth's special features, like the one begun below.

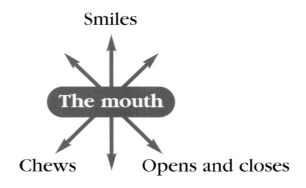

Smiles

The mouth

Chews   Opens and closes

   b) Choose the most interesting features from your diagram and **write two similes** for the mouth. For example, 'the mouth grinned like a trap shut tight.'

10 Unlike a simile, a metaphor does not compare one thing with another, but describes it as *being* another.

   a) Find the **metaphor** for the nose in the poem.

   b) Make up your own metaphor for the mouth, based on another feature from your spidergram. For example, 'A chewing monstrous creature, the mouth…'

Key Writing

 11 **a)** Write a **free verse poem** about the mouth that gobbles up the nose. Begin by making a short story plan based on the ideas below.

Introduction:	Imagine the mouth escapes the same day as the nose.
Complication:	Does it know where it's going? Does it encounter any problems along the way?
Crisis:	How does it solve the problem? Is it in danger? At what point does it eat the nose?
Resolution:	Does the mouth have the same fate as the nose or a different fate?

b) Next, give your poem some **structure**. If you find it helpful, begin by writing in sentences that you can change or break up into the lines of your poem. For example:

Sentence: Once upon a time there was a mouth.

Lines:
Once
there was a mouth.

Words left out

Lines of different lengths

c) Try to use some of the **similes and metaphors** you created in questions 9 and 10, to make the images in your poem more vivid.

③ Trick of the mind

Aims

▶ Read a series of explanations

▶ Learn how to separate description from explanation

▶ Learn the difference between the active and the passive

Derren Brown is a magician. Here he explains some of the secrets of the tricks shown in his television series.

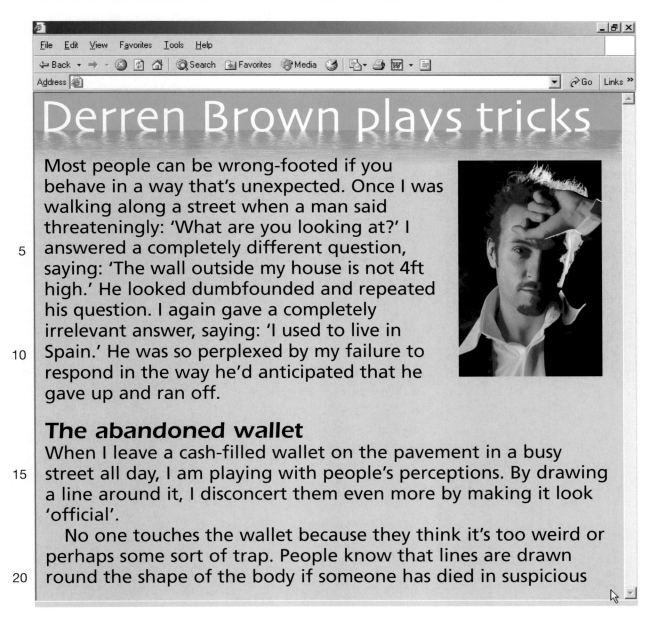

Derren Brown plays tricks

Most people can be wrong-footed if you behave in a way that's unexpected. Once I was walking along a street when a man said threateningly: 'What are you looking at?' I
5 answered a completely different question, saying: 'The wall outside my house is not 4ft high.' He looked dumbfounded and repeated his question. I again gave a completely irrelevant answer, saying: 'I used to live in
10 Spain.' He was so perplexed by my failure to respond in the way he'd anticipated that he gave up and ran off.

The abandoned wallet

When I leave a cash-filled wallet on the pavement in a busy
15 street all day, I am playing with people's perceptions. By drawing a line around it, I disconcert them even more by making it look 'official'.

No one touches the wallet because they think it's too weird or perhaps some sort of trap. People know that lines are drawn
20 round the shape of the body if someone has died in suspicious

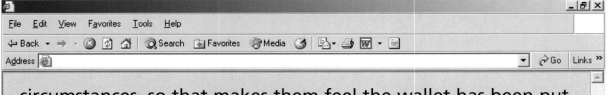

circumstances, so that makes them feel the wallet has been put there by the authorities. The line makes it clear that it's not lying there by accident.

25 I don't think the trick would work without the line around the wallet. It makes the object look surreal, as though it has been put there for some unknown purpose...

The aim of this trick of the mind is to make people feel so weird about picking up the wallet that they would rather play safe and not touch it. And it works!

30 ## Are you feeling sleepy?

All through the series, people mysteriously fall asleep in public phone boxes. Have they fallen prey to a disease or am I carrying out some trick of the mind on the other end of the line? There are two factors at work here.

35 First, the group of people subjected to the stunt are particularly suggestible. I know this simply because they chose to answer a public phone that happened to be ringing as they walked past. Most people would ignore it, assuming it was nothing to do with them.

40 Secondly, once the person answers, I immediately bombard them with a rapid set of confusing instructions and facts. I do this for several minutes without giving give them a break, then follow it by telling them to fall asleep. As seen on the shows, this works.

wrong-footed put (someone) in a difficult situation

dumbfounded amazed

disconcert upset, puzzle

surreal dreamlike, unreal

suggestible easily influenced by suggestion

bombard attack

Key Reading

Explanation texts

This text is mainly an **explanation**, but it also contains some **description**. Its **purpose** is to explain *how* something might work and *why* things happen.

The main features of this text are:

● It has a series of **clear and logical steps**. For example, in the second paragraph of the article, Derren Brown writes, 'By drawing a line around it, I disconcert them…'; this makes the first point of 'The abandoned wallet'.

● It uses the **present tense** when an explanation is being given. For example, '*I am playing with people's perceptions…*'

● It uses the **past tense** when describing how something has happened, for example, 'Once I *was walking* along the street when a man…'

● It uses **causal language**, which shows how one thing causes another, for example, 'No one touches the wallet *because…*'

● It uses **subheadings** when discussing different explanations. This makes the text easier to read.

1 What **kind of things** does Derren Brown explain in the text?

2 More than one tense is used in paragraph 1. Find an example of:
   ● the **present** tense
   ● the **past** tense.

3 What two **subheadings** are used in this article?

Purpose

4 What is the writer trying to **do** in this text? Choose from the following options:

- ● to demonstrate magic tricks
- ● to show that people are easily fooled
- ● to tell the reader why the tricks work.

Reading for meaning

Explanation texts can describe and explain, but not at the same time. For example, in paragraph 1 of the text the writer *describes* an incident.

Man confronts Derren Brown in street → Derren Brown talks nonsense → Man runs away.

In the lines 10–12, however, the writer *explains why* the man ran away.

> He was so perplexed by my failure to respond in the way he'd anticipated that he gave up and ran off.

You could reword the explanation like this:

> Derren Brown confused the man *so* the man ran away.

Or like this:

> The man ran away *because* Derren Brown confused him.

Remember, the connectives 'so' and 'because' show the link between cause and effect.

5 Working in groups, study lines 14–23.

a) First discuss what the **events** are. One person should **scan** the two paragraphs to gain this information.

R3

b) Another group member then sums up the events in **note form**, as shown on page 68. You should agree as a group how the notes are worded.

6 a) As a group read through the **summary** of events from question 5, and ask the question 'Why did people avoid the wallet?' Derren Brown gives several reasons in his explanation.

b) Now find the reasons given in the article and **discuss** them. Use expressions such as 'What about…?' and 'Does this mean…?' to help you.

Wr11

c) **Reword** Derren Brown's explanations to show the cause and effect, using the connectives 'so' or 'because'. For example, 'The line around the wallet makes it look official *so…*'

d) Choose a group member to **report back** with your summaries. Keep your notes safe for use in question 8.

. . . .

Focus on: The active and the passive

When Derren Brown describes his tricks, he often writes in the **active tense**. He is talking directly to the reader in an informal, chatty way. For example:

Who touches? No one. This is the **subject** of the sentence

Present tense **verb**

What do they not touch? The wallet. This is the **object** of the sentence

No one touches the wallet.

However, when Derren Brown *explains* the reasons why things happen, he sometimes uses the **passive** tense. It allows him to explain things in a more formal way. For example, the sentence 'No one touches the wallet' could be rewritten in the passive like this:

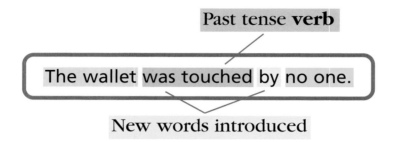

Past tense **verb**

The wallet was touched by no one.

New words introduced

7 Change the following sentences from the **passive to the active**:

a) Another trick was performed by Derren Brown.

b) They were all fooled by a fake séance.

c) The audience were convinced by the magic stunt.

Key Writing

8 Think back to the group work you did in questions 5 and 6. You are going to **rewrite** the section 'The abandoned wallet' in your own words, from memory.

● You will need to **describe the trick** and **explain** how it works. To help you, refer to your notes from questions 5 and 6 on the events and reasons behind the trick.

● Use **causal language** and **connectives** to show how cause and effect are linked in your explanation.

④ Unit 3 Assignment: The magician

 ## Assessment Focus

▶ **AF5** Vary sentences for clarity, purpose and effect

> **You:** are a magician with x-ray eyes.
>
> **Your task:** to write an explanation showing how a conjuring trick works.

Stage 1

Describing the trick

Read the description of the conjuring trick below.

> Ask six members of the audience to write a word on a sheet of paper, fold it in half, place it an envelope and seal it.
>
> 'With my x-ray eyes,' you say, 'I will read every word correctly!'
>
> To demonstrate your skill you pick up an envelope, show that your hands and sleeves are free, and with a flourish, lift the envelope to your x-ray eyes. Slowly you spell out the word. Someone in the audience gasps. You have spelled out their word.
>
> You pick up the next envelope. The same thing happens – and you work through each envelope spelling out each correct word.

Stage 2

Explaining the trick

Below are notes that explain the trick.

- You have an accomplice in the audience.
- You agree a word (for example, 'cabbage').
- Accomplice is given an envelope.
- Writes down 'cabbage'.
- You collect envelopes.
- Accomplice's envelope placed at bottom of pile.
- You pick up top envelope.
- Spell out 'cabbage'.
- Accomplice confirms the word and appears amazed.
- You open envelope, read aloud false word as 'cabbage'. But to yourself you read the word ('goat').
- You pick up another envelope.
- Spell out 'goat'.
- Confirmed by member of audience who wrote the word 'goat'.
- You open envelope, read aloud false word: 'goat'. But to yourself read the real word.
- And so on, to the last envelope.

Working with a partner, read the notes together and ensure that you understand them.

Stage 3

Write up the notes from Stage 2 as an explanation.

- Make a series of **clear points** in your explanation.

- Use the **first person** ('I') when referring to yourself. (Remember you are the magician.) Use the first person ('we') when referring to yourself and your accomplice.

- Write in the **present tense**.

- Use **causal connectives** to give reasons why the trick works, such as 'so' and 'because'.

Remember:

- Use connectives to help make the sequence of your explanation clear. For example:
  'First agree a word with your accomplice. Then...'

- Each line of the notes reads in the same way. To avoid this and make your explanation more interesting, you should vary your sentences. For example, use the active and the passive:
  Active: 'We agree a word.'
  Passive: 'A word is agreed by us.'

① Twister!

Aims

▷ Read an information text about tornadoes

▷ Examine the layout of a text

▷ Use the library and ICT to research and present information (R2)

▷ Write an information text (Wr10)

This text is from an information book for young people.

TORNADO ALLEY

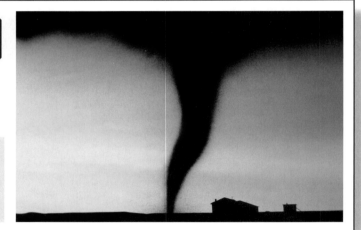

Tornadoes happen all over the world and are most common in North America, Europe, East Asia and Australia. In the United States, about 800 tornadoes are reported every year and around 70 people are killed. Waves of warm, moist air from the Gulf of Mexico often clash with cooler, dry winds
5 from the northern states of Canada and the Rocky Mountains. This clash leads to many tornadoes forming along a wide stretch of country through the states of Texas, Oklahoma, Kansas and Nebraska, which has earned the region the nickname of 'tornado alley'. Most of the region's twisters occur in April, May and June, and they account for over a third of all US tornadoes.
10 They usually occur during the afternoon or early evening, but there have been some night-time tornadoes. Florida is also often hit by tornadoes.

Twister!

It is no good trying to simply outrun a tornado – it will almost certainly catch-up with you. Anyone outside when a tornado approaches should try and move quickly away from the storm's path. If there is no time to escape the tornado's path, it is best to lie flat in the nearest ditch. Some houses in high-risk areas have an underground storm cellar for protection.

The Alley

An average of 125 tornadoes are reported in Texas every year, with over 50 in Oklahoma, 48 in Kansas and 38 in Nebraska. About ten people are killed by twisters every year in Texas alone. This map shows how tornadoes are swept in by warm winds off the Gulf of Mexico.

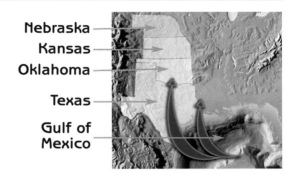

Nebraska
Kansas
Oklahoma
Texas
Gulf of Mexico

Toto

The National Severe Storms Laboratory is situated right in the middle of high-risk 'tornado alley' in Oklahoma. Scientists there have developed a barrel of instruments that can be dropped in a tornado's path to measure its temperature, air pressure, wind speed and direction. They call this the Totable Tornado Observatory – TOTO for short, after the name of the dog in *The Wonderful Wizard of Oz*. TOTO weighs 180kg (397lbs) and is transported on the back of a special pick-up lorry.

Bermuda Triangle

In the seas of the Atlantic Ocean between Bermuda, Florida and Puerto Rico, there is a mysterious area known as the Bermuda Triangle. Many ships and planes have disappeared here without trace. In 1945 a squadron of five US planes on a training mission vanished at the same time, and a search plane sent out to look for them also went missing. More than 50 ships are said to have disappeared in the region. One theory is that they were lost in storms, especially waterspouts, in that area.

Texan Twister

Texas suffers more tornadoes than any other state in the USA. On 11 May 1953, a single tornado hit Waco in central Texas, just 300 km (186 miles) from the coast of the Gulf of Mexico, killing 114 people. The worst US tragedy happened in 1925, when a group of tornadoes hit the states of Missouri, Illinois and Indiana, killing a total of 689 people.

storm cellar underground shelter, often equipped with supplies and first aid equipment
squadron unit in the Air Force of two or more flights of aircraft

Key Reading

Information texts

This text is mainly an **information** text. Its **purpose** is to give clear information about a topic.

The main features of this text are:

● It uses verbs in the **present tense** when it is telling things as they are, for example, *'800 tornadoes are reported every year…'*

● It uses verbs in the **past tense** when providing details of past events, for example, *'One theory is that they were lost in storms…'*

● Its **layout** includes photos and maps to attract the reader's attention and present information visually.

● It uses **headings** and **subheadings** to make it easier to find information, for example, information on tornadoes in Texas is given under the subheading *'Texan Twister'*.

● It includes both **general information** and **specific facts**, often described using technical language. For example,
General fact: *'Tornadoes happen all over the world…'*
Specific fact: *'(scientific instruments) measure… temperature, air pressure, wind speed and direction.'*

1 Find three examples of the **present tense** in paragraph 1.

2 When is the text written in the **past tense** and why? Find an example.

3 Identify **two specific facts**, using technical language.

4 **a)** What kinds of **visual information** are included in the text? Find two different examples.

   b) What part of the text does each example refer to? Write down the **subheadings**.

Purpose

Although the main purpose of this text is to give information on tornadoes, it also contains an explanation.

5 **a)** Where does the **explanation begin** in paragraph 1?

b) What is it about? Write down the **words** that tell you.

Reading for meaning

The layout of an information text helps to guide the reader. It is not simply there to look attractive. It allows the reader to browse the page. You do not need to begin at the beginning and read each paragraph. Instead, you can easily select the parts you want to read.

6 Look at the text and note as many features as you can that aid reading. Think about:

- the **headings**
- the **font** or typeface
- the different kinds of **visual information**.

7 **a)** Read the following paragraph again. It contains several **facts**.

The Alley

An average of 125 tornadoes are reported in Texas every year, with over 50 in Oklahoma, 48 in Kansas and 38 in Nebraska. About ten people are killed by twisters every year in Texas alone.

b) Work out a way of laying out this information as a **simple chart**. Think about how many columns and rows you will need.

c) What information is **missing** from the paragraph that would complete your chart?

This information text also contains advice.

8 Paragraph 2 offers three pieces of **advice** to someone caught in the path of a tornado. Find this advice.

• •

Focus on: Carrying out research

You can find more information about tornadoes by researching in books or through databases. A database is a way of storing facts in a list or table on a computer.

Which method would give you the best information? This depends on what you want to know. For example, if you want specific facts about tornadoes, a database would be the best method. You can find these on CD-ROMs or websites.

R2

9 a) Read the section 'Texan Twister' again. Then, **with your teacher's guidance**, carry out **ICT research** using suitable databases to find out the following about tornadoes in Texas:
- some of the most severe tornadoes
- when these took place
- the wind speed of the tornadoes
- the damage to homes and crops.

Use a **search engine** effectively to help you and remember to include key words in each search question. For example, if you leave out the word 'Texas' you will not get the information you want.

b) Create a document of the most interesting facts organised under subheadings, for use in question 10.

Key Writing

Wr10 **10** **a)** Using ICT, write an **opening statement** about tornadoes for a young person's information text. Include:

- some of the facts you have researched about tornadoes in Texas

- any facts from the 'Tornado Alley' text that interest you.

Either key this opening statement straight into a document *or* write a rough draft, correct it and then key in the final draft.

b) Next, **construct a table** using the factual information from your research. Follow these instructions:

> **1** Provide a heading for your table.
>
> **2** Click on the 'Insert Table' icon and choose the correct number of columns and rows.
> *or*
> Click on 'Table Menu' then click on 'Insert'.
>
> **3** Key in the correct number of columns and rows.
>
> **4** Cut and paste the facts and figures from your research document into your table.

c) Print out your completed page or **save** in your own folder.

② Bee attack

Aims

‣ Read a report about an attack by bees
‣ Record events in chronological order (S6)
‣ Use powerful verbs (W11)
‣ Write a report

The following account from *Tea Pests* by J.W. Beagle-Atkins tells the amazing story of an attack by a swarm of bees. These are highly fierce tree bees related to hornets and any attack would be serious. The events are told by the victim, who is out riding at the time.

Buzzing Death

Souvenir jumped, bucked, reared and lashed out in all directions to rid himself of the bees, while I, attempting to protect my face and limbs,
5   had the greatest difficulty in retaining my saddle. In a few moments, an angry buck while turning a corner at full gallop threw me into the dust.

    With less than a mile to safety, I began to leg it with far greater
10   determination than I had ever done in my life. But I was covered from head to foot with bees; they crawled in thousands all over me, stinging with excruciating pain. The under-rim of my topee became an angry hive, bees clustered inches deep. My forehead, ears and neck were blanketed in a buzzing, stinging swab of agony. Bees crawled inside my
15   open-necked shirt and up my unprotecting shorts; they were everywhere. I tore them away in handfuls, but only to make room for others about me in clouds.

As I staggered on I yelled frantically to distant workers; but seeing the swarms about me, they bolted in every direction but
20 mine. Gasping for breath, each time I opened my swollen mouth, more bees entered, until my tongue was stung to twice its normal size, and I was crunching them with my teeth. My nostrils had swollen into uselessness; my eyes, stung and running with water, were rapidly closing…

25 …My timely rescue was effected by two quick-witted Gurkhas, who had raced to a thatch stack and, bringing bundles of dry grass, had quickly surrounded me with a dense wall of fire and smoke, until the bees were beaten off. Later, as I lay unconscious, while the district was being scoured for a
30 doctor, these same two staunch men insisted upon remaining and extracting stings from my inflamed carcass. It took two days to free my body of the discarded stings. When, eventually, I recovered consciousness I was beamingly informed that I had had at least two thousand punctures, probably a record.

35 I lay in torment for several days, unable to move. My body, blown up like an oversized sausage, was black, blue and purple, and as hard as frozen meat. For several days I could see and speak only with the greatest difficulty, and it took many applications of anti-swelling lotions before what had once been
40 my nose and ears again emerged from the general mess.

My convalescence was a lengthy business of some six months in the hospital and several weeks in the cool hills of Darjeeling.

---

buck a vertical jump made by a horse
excruciating very painful
topee type of hat, a pith helmet
Gurkhas people from Nepal known for being good soldiers
carcass the dead body of an animal
convalescence the gradual recovery of health after an illness
Darjeeling a hill town in West Bengal

Key Reading

Recount texts

This text is a **recount** or **chronological report**. Its **purpose** is to recount or tell the reader about a series of events in the order in which they happened.

The main features of this text are:

- It is told in the **past tense**, for example, '*I yelled…*'
- It describes events in **time order** (chronological order), for example, we are told that the writer's recovery after the attack '*took some six months…*'
- It uses **time connectives**, for example, '*Later, as I lay unconscious…*'

1 a) Over what **period** did the events described in the text happen – a week, a month or longer?

b) What happens to the writer by the end of the text?

2 What **tense** is the text written in?

3 a) Is the text written in the **first person** or the **third person**?

b) How can you tell that this text is from an **autobiography**?

Grammar for reading

An **autobiography** is the story of someone's life, written by that person.

Purpose

4 What is the **main purpose** of this text? Did the author write it:

- because he survived the attack
- to entertain the reader with a gripping event
- to warn the reader about the dangers of bees
- to thank the Gurkhas for their help?

Point to evidence in the text to support your answer.

Reading for meaning

Chronological order

A lot happens in the recount *Buzzing Death*, and many details are given. This can make it difficult to pick out the main events. However, it is written in chronological order, like a story/narrative. This means you can sum up the events in each paragraph on a timeline. The first event has been added to start you off.

The writer is attacked by a swarm of bees.

S6

5 Sum up the **main events** of *Buzzing Death* and add them along your own version of the timeline. **Follow these steps** for each paragraph:

- Read the paragraph again.
- Picture in your mind what is happening.
- Sum this up in one or two sentences.
- Record these sentences on the timeline.

For example, you are told in paragraph 1 that the pony, Souvenir, began to panic. What else happens?

> In a few moments, an angry buck while turning a corner at full gallop threw me into the dust.

So the main event is: 'His pony threw him into the dust'. You would write this as the next event on your timeline.

6 When your timeline is finished, **bracket** the events that happened **during** the attack and those that happened **after** the attack, as in the example below:

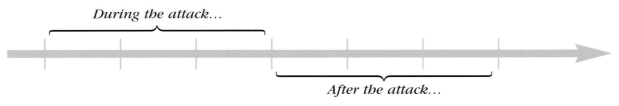

During the attack…

After the attack…

. . . .

Focus on: Creating images

The writer brings his recount to life with vivid word pictures or images. For example, when the bees are attacking in paragraphs 1, 2 and 3, he creates an image of the attack using powerful verbs.

In line 1 he could have said:

> Souvenir *jumped* in all directions…

Instead he says:

> Souvenir *jumped, bucked, reared* and *lashed out* in all directions…

These verbs tell the reader just how awful the experience was and give a strong impression of the pony's actions. They also tell the reader how the writer felt.

7 Below are further verbs from the text.

| blanketed | crawled | staggered | yelled | bolted | tore |

a) Use a thesaurus to **find synonyms** (words that have similar meanings) to these words.

W11

b) Record them in a list, for example:
blanketed – enveloped, covered

Key Writing

R3

8 a) Imagine that you are attacked by a plague of biting insects, such as mosquitoes. Draw up a table with the following column headings and **make short notes** under each one. The first column has been started for you.

Before the attack	During the attack	After the attack
A cloud of mosquitoes approach		
No time to take cover		

b) Use your notes to **write a recount** of three paragraphs about the attack. Each paragraph should be about 50 words long.

- Use the first person 'I'.
- Write in the past tense.
- Include powerful verbs to describe what is happening. Choose the best from the list you created for question 7.

You could start the first paragraph like this:

'Everyone looked up, pointing into the distance. The sky was dense, crammed full with...'

③ The Birds

- Read an extract from a short story
- Learn ways of extending sentences
- Study the different styles used in the text (S10)
- Discuss in groups, predicting what might happen (S&L11)

The following extract is from the short story _The Birds_ by Daphne du Maurier. Nat, a farm worker, and his family live in a small cottage. Autumn has suddenly turned into a bitterly cold winter and during the night some birds have entered the children's bedroom. Earlier they attacked Nat at the window.

'What is it, Nat, what's happened?' his wife called from the further bedroom, and swiftly he pushed the children through the door to the passage and shut it upon them, so that he was alone now, in their bedroom, with the birds.

5   He seized a blanket from the nearest bed, and using it as a weapon flung it to right and left about him in the air. He felt the thud of bodies, heard the fluttering of wings, but they were not yet defeated, for again and again they returned to the assault, jabbing his hands, his head, the little stabbing beaks sharp as a

10   pointed fork. The blanket became a weapon of defence; he wound it about his head, and then in greater darkness beat at the birds with his bare hands. He dared not stumble to the door and open it, lest in doing so the birds should follow him.

How long he fought with them in the darkness he could not tell, but at least the beating of the wings about him lessened and then withdrew, and through the density of the blanket he was aware of light. He waited, listened; there was no sound except the fretful crying of the children from the bedroom beyond. The fluttering, the whirring of the wings had ceased.

He took the blanket from him and stared about him. The cold grey morning light exposed the room. Dawn, and the open window, had called the living birds; the dead lay on the floor. Nat gazed at the little corpses, shocked and horrified. They were all small birds, none of any size; there must have been fifty of them lying there upon the floor. There were robins, finches, sparrows, blue tits, larks and bramblings, birds that by nature's law kept to their own flock and their own territory, and now, joining one with another in their urge for battle, had destroyed themselves against the bedroom walls, or in the strife had been destroyed by him. Some had lost feathers in the fight, others had blood, his blood, upon their beaks…

Later that day Nat returns home from the farm to find that there has been a government announcement over the radio. His wife, Jill, has written it down.

'Statement from the Home Office at eleven a.m. today. Reports from all over the country are coming in hourly about the vast quantity of birds flocking above towns, villages and outlying districts, causing obstructions and damage and even attacking individuals. It is thought that the Arctic air stream, at present covering the British Isles, is causing birds to migrate south in immense numbers, and that intense hunger may drive these birds to attack human beings. Householders are warned to see to their windows, doors and chimneys, and to take reasonable precautions for the safety of their children. A further statement will be issued later.'

lest in case (used to stop something happening)
bramblings finches
Arctic air stream air current coming from the North Pole

Key Reading

Narrative texts

This text is an extract from a **narrative**. Its **purpose** is to tell a story in an entertaining way.

The main features of this text are:

● It has a structure that includes an opening (**introduction**), a problem (**complication**), a dramatic moment when everything comes to a head (**crisis**) and an ending (**resolution**) when things are sorted out. For example, this text comes from the middle of the story. A complication has arisen (the birds begin to attack) and the story is building to the crisis.

● It has **characters**, who the story is about. We often hear their words and thoughts.

● There is also a **narrator**, who tells the story in either the first person (I/we) or the third person (he/she/it). For example, '*swiftly he pushed the children through the door…*'

● It uses **powerful words**. The language of the narrative must be interesting to read or listen to. For example, '*He felt the thud of bodies, heard the fluttering of wings…*'

1 a) How does the text **open**? Check the first sentence.

b) What **tense** is used in this sentence?

2 Is the story told in the **first** or the **third person**?

3 What important **information** is the reader given at the end of the extract?

· ·

Purpose

The purpose of a narrative is to entertain the reader. One way to do this is by catching and keeping the reader's interest. For example, the extract opens with the question: '*What is it, Nat, what's happened?*'. This shows that at least one of the characters is unaware of what's going on and this makes the reader want to know more.

4 What **action** follows straight after this piece of speech?

5 At what point in paragraph 1 does the reader find out what the **problem** is?

· ·

Reading for meaning

The Birds is a short story full of description. Many sentences are long and packed with detail. For example, lines 6–10 describe Nat alone in the room with the birds:

> He felt the thud of bodies, heard the fluttering of wings, but they were not yet defeated, for again and again they returned to the assault, jabbing his hands, his head, the little stabbing beaks sharp as a pointed fork.

When reading this long sentence, vivid pictures come tumbling out one after the other. However, if the sentence was split up into smaller sentences, some of the pace and excitement would be lost. The series of actions that make up the fight would be broken. For example:

Pauses mean that the sentence loses pace

He felt the thud of bodies, heard the fluttering of wings. *But* they were not yet defeated. *Again* and again they returned to the assault. *They* jabbed his hands, his head, the little stabbing beaks sharp as a pointed fork.

6 Try turning the following two short sentences into one **long sentence**. You will need to use a connective such as 'but', 'so' or 'and' and alter the punctuation to match.

The birds kept pecking at his arms and his head. Time and again he fought them off with the blanket.

Extending sentences

One way in which the writer extends sentences is by using the '-ing' form of the verb. For example, *'they returned to the assault, jabbing his hands, his head…'*

You can do this in your own writing by changing different verbs. For example, 'It plunged down. It struck the floor with a clatter' could become: 'Plunging down, it struck the floor with a clatter' or 'It plunged down, striking the floor with a clatter.'

7 **Write a short paragraph** about a bird (or another wild creature) trapped in a room. Include '-ing' verbs at the beginning and middle of sentences. You could use some of the following verbs:

diving   crawling   colliding   crushing

• •

Focus on: Change of style

The final paragraph of the extract is a bulletin from the government warning the country about the attacking birds. It is written in a direct, formal style with few images. This is quite different from the style of the earlier paragraphs. For example, the passive tense is used to stress the formal tone:

'It is *thought* that…'

The active tense would be less formal:

'We think the *Arctic* air stream…'

There are also other features that emphasise the direct, formal style of the bulletin.

S10 **8** **a)** What **tense** is the bulletin written in?

b) How does this **contrast** with the tense used in the earlier paragraphs?

9 What **technical vocabulary** is used in the bulletin? Find two examples and explain their meanings.

10 What **kind of text** would you say the bulletin is mainly? (Think about its purpose.) Is it:

- a recount
- an information text
- an explanation
- a narrative?

> **Grammar for reading**
>
> In **active** sentences, the subject performs the action on the object, for example, 'Police arrested the burglar.' In **passive** sentences, the subject is on the receiving end of the action, for example, 'The burglar was arrested by the police.'

Key Speaking and Listening

11 **a)** A second bulletin is broadcast from the government later in the story. It begins:

'This is London…'

Working in a small group, discuss what you think the bulletin will say. Here are some questions to consider:

- Will the government have control of the situation?
- Will the bird attacks have got worse?
- Will the situation be out of control?
- What will happen to Nat? Will he save the day?

S&L11

Share your ideas in the group, listening to and then building on what each person says. For example, if someone comments that the government will have control of the situation, ask 'How?'

b) Choose a group member to **make brief notes** of your ideas for what the bulletin will contain, as you go along.

c) Select a group member to **report your ideas** for the bulletin to another group, explaining how you made your decisions. How do the two groups' ideas compare?

④ Unit 4 Assignment: The weather forecaster

Assessment Focus

▶ AF2 Produce texts which are appropriate to task, reader and purpose

---

You: are a US weather forecaster.

Your task: to write an information leaflet about tornadoes in the USA which includes safety advice.

· ·

Stage 1

First **plan the layout** of your leaflet.

● What kind of heading will you give your leaflet?

● Where will you position any subheadings?

● What other layout features will you include?

(You should draw on the work you did on tornadoes earlier in the unit.)

Start with an **opening paragraph** giving general information on the nature of tornadoes and detailed examples. Use the notes on the next page and any other information you collected on tornadoes earlier in the unit.

- travels from the Gulf of Mexico
- paths and danger zones (for example, Tornado Alley)
- speed
- time of year they occur
- tornado may change direction
- TOTO.

Stage 2

Next, include a section giving information on the importance of having access to a storm cellar. Give this section a clear **subheading**.

Use these notes to help form your main points:

- permanent storm cellar – a windowless room
- equipped with essentials: drinking water, food, first aid kit, torch, radio
- difference between a 'warning' and a 'watch' (the first means a tornado is on the way, the second a tornado is suspected)
- ensure everyone is present in an emergency – all the family, neighbours, pets

Stage 3

Write the information leaflet following your plan. Remember to:

- use the present tense for presenting things as they are
- use the past tense when describing past events
- expand your sentences, starting with a general point and illustrating with specific facts.

Challenge

Turn some of the information in Stage 2 into advice by using imperative verbs and bullet points instead of a full paragraph. For example:

'Storm cellars need to be equipped with food, drink...'

becomes:

'Make sure your storm cellar is equipped with...'

① Billy and his father

Aims

- Read an extract from a film script
- Explore the features of film scripts
- Develop drama skills and techniques (S&L14)
- Explore character, relationships and issues (S&L16)

This extract is from the film script for *Billy Elliot* by Lee Hall. It is about a boy named Billy from north-east England, whose father is a miner. Billy wants to be a ballet dancer, but his family are very poor.

```
      INT. ELLIOT HOUSE.
      DAD'S BEDROOM - DAY.
      We see DAD looking at
      Mum's jewellery.

5     CUT TO:
      EXT. PAWNSHOP - NEWCASTLE
      DAD walks towards the pawnshop.
      He opens the door and goes in.

      CUT TO:
10    EXT. STREET - DAY
      DAD and BILLY walk down the road. Dad
      carries a suitcase. Billy dances.
         DAD     Is that absolutely necessary?
                 Walk normal, will you.

15    CUT TO:
      INT. BUS. MOTORWAY - later
      BILLY and DAD sit on the bus.
```

pawnshop a shop where people are given money in return for their valuable things. They have to pay the money back within a certain time to regain their things

audition a test of performance skills to see whether you will be selected

Billy looks out at the motorway.

BILLY	So what's it like, like?
20	DAD	What's what like?
BILLY	London.
DAD	I don't know, son.
	I never made it past Durham.
25	BILLY	Have you never been, like?
DAD	Why would I want to go to London?
BILLY	Well, it's the Capital City.
DAD	Well, there's no mines in London.
BILLY	Christ, is that all you think about?

CUT TO:

30 EXT. MOTORWAY – AFTERNOON
From outside the bus we see BILLY look out. The bus becomes a blur as it races past us.

CUT TO:

EXT. ROYAL BALLET SCHOOL – DAY
35 *DAD and BILLY walk towards the school.*

CUT TO:

INT. ENTRANCE TO ROYAL BALLET SCHOOL – DAY
A RECEPTIONIST is sitting at a desk. BILLY and DAD enter.

40	RECEP	Can I help you?
DAD	Billy Elliot. We've come for an audition.
RECEP	Oh, you mean William Elliot.
DAD	Yeah, William.
RECEP	Ah yes. Can you go upstairs, please?
45 *Dad glances at the stairs.*
DAD	This way?
RECEP	Yes.
DAD	Thanks.

They climb the stairs.

50

INT. ROYAL BALLET SCHOOL. CHANGING ROOM – DAY
BILLY walks in past some other boys, SIMON and JOHN.

SIMON	This your first time?
JOHN	Yeah.
SIMON	Cor, I've been doing this for two years
55		now.
	(to Billy) Hello. Nerve-racking isn't it?
	Where are you from?
BILLY	Everington. County Durham.
SIMON	Durham? Isn't there an amazing cathedral?
60 | BILLY | Dunno. Never been. |

Key Reading

Film scripts

This text is a **film script**. Its **purpose** is to provide a written version of a film for those involved in the film, such as the actors and the director.

The main features of this text are:

- The **layout** is set on the page in a special way. For example, the names of the characters are separated from the speech, there are no speech marks and the layout includes information about locations. For example, 'INT' means 'interior' (inside) and 'EXT' means 'exterior' (outside).

- It contains **visual information/directions** to actors. For example, camera instructions like 'Cut to' or 'DAD walks towards the pawnshop. He opens the door and goes in.'

- It has **dialogue/speech** which is often in quite **short sentences**, for example:
  ```
  SIMON  This your first time?
  JOHN   Yeah.
  ```

1 In the film, Billy, a boy from a poor mining community in north-east England, decides he wants to be a ballet dancer. Why do you think this might make a **good story**?

2 Exactly where are Billy and his father going?

3 Find an example of an **exterior location** and an **interior location** in the first few lines of the script.

4 Find at least one other piece of **visual information** that describes what a character does.

Purpose

Lee Hall's purpose in writing this film script is to tell a great story. Most good stories need **conflict**. This happens when characters disagree, argue, or even fight.

Conflict occurs in *Billy Elliot* partly because Billy's father and brother don't think it is 'manly' to be a ballet dancer. Here is a short extract from earlier in the script:

```
BILLY   I don't see what's wrong with it.
DAD     You know perfectly well what's wrong with it.
BILLY   No, I don't.
DAD     Yes, you do.
BILLY   No, I don't.
DAD     Yes, you bloody well do. Who do you think I am?
```

5 In pairs, **read these lines** together. Do it in two different ways:

S&L14

   a) First, read it with Billy being quiet and a little frightened, and Dad being angry.

   b) Then read it with both Billy and Dad getting angrier and louder.

6 The scene is set in the kitchen and Billy and his father are sitting down. Imagine that one of them bangs his fist on the table during the argument. Decide **who** might make this gesture and **at what point** in the argument.

7 Now **act out the scene** and include the gesture. Does adding this gesture change the way the scene works?

Reading for meaning

8 The reader learns quite a lot about Billy and his father from the extract on pages 96 and 97. Find **evidence** in the script of the things listed in column 1 of the table below. Then **copy the table** and complete column 2, following the first example.

What the reader finds out	Evidence
Billy's father does not have much money.	Billy's father takes his wife's jewellery to the pawnshop.
Billy's father still finds it difficult to accept that Billy likes dancing.	
Billy's father doesn't have much experience of travel.	
Billy is very different from the other boys at the audition.	

Script writers often put themselves in the position of the cinema audience. In this example from the extract, it is as if we are watching the film.

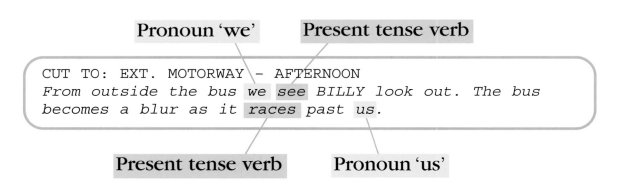

Pronoun 'we'   Present tense verb

CUT TO: EXT. MOTORWAY – AFTERNOON
From outside the bus we see BILLY look out. The bus becomes a blur as it races past us.

Present tense verb   Pronoun 'us'

9 **Write your own scene direction** to go with the short extract on page 99.

● Use the pronoun 'we'.

● Use the present tense.

Imagine the camera is looking through the window into Billy's kitchen. For example, *'From outside the house, we see…'*

Focus on: Creating dramatic performances

10 a) On your own, reread the last section of the extract when Billy arrives at the Royal Ballet, (lines 33–61).

b) In a group, agree how you think each of the characters in the extract should behave. Complete a chart like the one below, so that you have a record of what your group decides.

Character	What he or she is like	How can this be shown?
Receptionist	A snob?	Peers over her glasses at Billy and his dad.
Dad	Nervous	
Billy		

Key Speaking and Listening

11 a) In the same groups as for question 10, **perform the script extract**. You will need to decide:
- who will read each part
- who will read the directions and actions.

Use your notes from question 10 to guide your performance.

b) When you have finished your performance, **discuss how it went**.
- Was the relationship between Billy and his dad clear?
- Did the other people in the extract have clear, convincing characters?
- How successful did you think your group's performance was overall?

12 Now, working on your own, write up your thoughts as a **short commentary** of approximately 75 words. You could begin like this:

> I thought our group performed the scene quite...
>
> This was because...

2 Writing for *The Simpsons*

Aims

◗ Read about a script writer for a famous TV programme

◗ Look at how a key idea is developed in a text (R5)

◗ Explore different ways of organising sentences within paragraphs (S6)

One of the most well-known family TV programmes is *The Simpsons*. But how does it get written and who are the writers? This text is about the only female writer on the team and how she came to write for the show.

Writing for *The Simpsons*

When *The Simpsons* writers start to argue about storylines, one voice stands out from the rest – the only woman on the team, Carolyn Omine. But Omine admits she's not afraid to shout as loud and as hard as the boys. After three years writing for the award-winning show she's got used to fighting her corner
5 in the testosterone-loaded atmosphere.

She says: "When I come out with a really nasty joke, I sometimes feel like I'm not the most feminine person in the world. I feel like I go back to being a girl when I get into my own office again."

10   Emmy Award-winning Omine had spent eight years as a writer on comedy shows in the US before she landed the job with *The Simpsons*. And she had always been so desperate to work on the show, that in all her previous contracts she had insisted on a clause that said she would be freed immediately if she was ever offered the chance to work on an episode.

15   "Everyone always agreed because they thought there was no chance," she laughs.

Her big chance came when she was recommended to one of the show's executive producers by his brother, who she had been working with. "It was staffing season, which is the time of year when you have to get a job if you're a writer otherwise you're unemployed for a year.

20   "I had an interview with *The Simpsons*, then it was a month until I heard if I'd got it. I hadn't been offered anything else and I thought for the first time I might be unemployed."

Although she is the only woman writer on the show, she admits that's not rare in US TV comedy. "In everything I've worked on I've always been the only
25   woman, or one of two. I don't think it's about prejudice, I just think there are not so many women trying to be comedy writers.

"Only five per cent of the job is sitting writing a script. You sometimes spend 12 hours a day sitting round a table with the guys shouting over them to be heard. I don't think a lot of women would be comfortable doing that. And I
30   think boys are encouraged far more than girls to be funny."

Writing for *The Simpsons* is very much a team effort. Scripts are put together eight months before the show is screened but there's a lot of tinkering after that and changes are made right up to the last minute to ensure each episode is topical. The stories start with ideas brought in by the writers. Unlike other US
35   TV shows, the network and studio are not allowed to dictate plots or themes in a deal that was thrashed out when *The Simpsons* first began.

testosterone a male hormone, which has been linked to aggression
clause section in a contract
prejudice unfair treatment
dictate tell people what to do without discussion

Key Reading

Recount texts

This text is mainly a **recount**. Its **purpose** is to tell the reader about events in someone's life. However, it also **explains** how certain things are done.

The main features of this text are:

- It describes someone's **past life**. This part is written in the **past tense** and told in **time order** (chronological order). For example, *'Her big chance came when…'*

- It describes **continuing situations** (for example, what Omine does now). These parts use the **present tense**. For example, *'You sometimes spend 12 hours a day sitting round a table…'*

- It includes references to **time** and uses **time connectives**. For example, *'Omine had spent eight years as a writer…'*, *'…the time of year when you have to get a job.'*

1 a) What is Carolyn Omine's **current job**?

   b) In what way is she **unusual**?

2 **How long** did Omine have to wait after her interview with *The Simpsons* team before she was told if she had got the job?

3 Find another example of a **time connective** in paragraph 2.

Purpose

This text has several purposes because it deals with several things.

4 Here are some possible reasons why the text was written. Find **evidence** for these reasons in the extract. Then **complete the sentences** below.

Purpose 1: To tell us about Carolyn Omine's life as a writer.

Evidence: It is clear that the writer is keen to tell us about Omine's life because...

Purpose 2: To tell us about how scripts for *The Simpsons* get written.

Evidence: We can see that the text is about how the scripts get written because...

Reading for meaning

Another purpose the writer of this text might have is to tell people how difficult it is for a woman writing on a comedy show. This idea can be followed through the text: there are four paragraphs where comments are made about Omine being a woman writer for *The Simpsons.*

R5

5 Find the four paragraphs and note down the first and last word of each one. For example:

Reference 1: Paragraph starting: 'When the Simpsons writers...'

Paragraph ending: '...testosterone-loaded atmosphere.'

6 How does Omine **feel** about working with so many men? Is she put off by it?

Focus on: Organising sentences in paragraphs

7 **How many sentences** does the following paragraph contain?

> Writing for *The Simpsons* is very much a team effort. Scripts are put together eight months before the show is screened but there's a lot of tinkering after that and changes are made right up to the last minute to ensure each episode is topical.

Now let's look at how these sentences work:

● The sentence 'Writing for *The Simpsons* is very much a team effort' is like an **introduction** (giving a general idea).

● It introduces the next sentence, which gives further details.

S6

8 What **difference** does it make if you move the first sentence after the second sentence?

Now look at the highlighted sentence in the paragraph below. See how it links back to the previous two sentences.

> When *The Simpsons* writers start to argue about storylines, one voice stands out from the rest – the only woman on the team, Carolyn Omine. But Omine admits she's not afraid to shout as loud and as hard as the boys. *After three years writing for the award-winning show she's got used to fighting her corner in the testosterone-loaded atmosphere.*

The reader knows what show this is because it was mentioned earlier

The pronoun 'she' is fine here because she (Carolyn) has been mentioned earlier

9 In pairs, discuss whether or not you could move the sentence in italics to another place in the paragraph without changing the meaning.

Key Writing

10 Now try **organising a paragraph** for yourself. Use **no more than two** of the sentences from the list below to make your paragraph.

- Millions of people around the world tune in every week to watch *The Simpsons*.

- *The Simpsons* is an incredibly popular show.

- Some people never miss an episode and have even cancelled weddings to catch a new one!

- People will do anything to watch *The Simpsons*.

a) Make sure the **first** sentence of your paragraph introduces a **general** idea.

b) Your **second** sentence should expand on your first sentence by giving further **details**.

③ My Family

Aims

▶ Read a review of a television programme

▶ Explore and revise features of reviews

▶ Write part of your own review (Wr18)

My Family is a situation comedy about an English family. The following text is a preview of the My Family Christmas 'special'.

Top TV

My Family brings humour to Christmas Day

My Family, on the BBC, is probably one of my favourite comedy shows of recent years. No matter what the episode, I always end up laughing 5 out loud at the bizarre antics and funny one-liners that issue forth from the Harper family.

And this year's Christmas Day episode is no different. The Harpers, minus Janie, have been out Christmas shopping in 10 London, and are on the Tube, in a tunnel. The train is stuck, for reasons that are never quite clear, providing ample

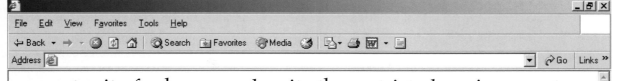

opportunity for humour despite the restricted environment. Indeed, the close confines give the actors a chance to really be their characters, with relatively little else to interact with
15 | beyond each other. It is as if they've been placed on an empty stage and told to get on with it.

Nick is as stupidly funny as ever, scaring an old woman by suggesting their situation is just like the start of "Cannibal Holocaust". He later sells water to the desperate passengers,
20 | all the while denying it to his own father. Ben is as pessimistic as ever, in that hugely funny way that he has. Susan attempts to become the leader of carriage 7, embarrassing herself and her family in the bargain before insulting the driver, who promptly refuses to move the train. Michael goes on several
25 | dates with a girl from a few carriages down the train, again showcasing the zaniness of his family by refusing to have anything to do with their world.

As we watch and laugh out loud, we can perhaps give thanks that this isn't our family, and enjoy a well-scripted
30 | and acted episode that leaves you hanging on for season five of this wonderful comedy.

pessimistic expects the worst
showcases highlights

Key Reading

Reviews

This text is a **review** of a television programme. Its **purpose** is to inform the reader about the programme, and give an opinion of how good or bad it is.

The main features of this text are:

● It provides **key information** about the story and characters. For example, Character:'*Nick is as stupidly funny as ever*'; Story:'*The Harpers, minus Janie, have been out Christmas shopping in London*'.

● It gives the reader an idea of what the reviewer's **opinion** is, through the words and phrases selected. For example, in '*one of my favourite comedy shows*', the adjective 'favourite' reveals how much the writer likes it.

● It mainly uses the **present tense**, even though the reviewer has already seen the programme. For example: '*Michael goes on several dates with a girl*'.

● It uses **sentences packed with detail** to give as much information as possible. For example,

'Susan attempts to become the leader of carriage 7, embarrassing herself and her family in the bargain before insulting the driver, who promptly refuses to move the train.'

Note the **three separate sections** of information following the introductory part (the first clause).

1 Does the **title** of the review give us any clue about what the reviewer thinks of the programme? How?

2 Can you find other examples of **key information** in the review? What are you told about Ben in paragraph 3, for example?

3 Identify one other sentence that is **packed with detail** from paragraph 3.

Purpose

Clearly, the writer wants the reader to share her enthusiasm for the programme. She does this by:

- mentioning some of the funny moments from the story
- encouraging the reader (through her language) to watch the programme.

4 In the last paragraph, the writer says five **positive things** about the show. Look for what she says about:

- laughter
- what it makes us think about her own family
- the acting and writing
- a phrase meaning 'waiting impatiently'
- a word meaning 'fantastic' or 'great'.

Reading for meaning

The characters in the programme are described in two ways. On the one hand, the reviewer uses very simple descriptions, such as:

Nick is stupidly funny…

Ben is as pessimistic as ever…

When it comes to Susan, however, you have to work out what sort of person she is from what she does.

5 Read this information about Susan. Then **write down four words** to describe her.

> Susan attempts to become the leader of carriage 7, embarrassing herself and her family in the bargain before insulting the driver, who promptly refuses to move the train.

Focus on: Recognising bias and objectivity

It is natural to expect a review of a TV programme to have an opinion – and be 'biased' one way or the other. In fact, it is almost impossible for a reviewer to be **objective**. It is especially difficult with a television comedy, because what makes each viewer laugh will be different.

> **Grammar for reading**
>
> To be **objective** is to be able make comments or decisions without allowing your feelings to get in the way of facts or the truth.

6 What TV programmes make you laugh? **Talk with a partner** about them and try to say what it is that you find funny. Say something about:
- the situations
- the storylines.

Now look at the two extracts from reviews of *My Family*.

> *Review 1:*
> The Christmas episode takes place on a tube train. Ben, Susan, Nick and younger brother Michael are all trapped on it, and they each try to get through it in different ways.

> *Review 2:*
> This rather stupid Christmas episode takes place on a tube train – how original! Ben – irritating and unfunny, Susan – even more irritating, and Nick (completely unbeleivable) are stuck on a train, along with Michael, the youngest child in the Harper family.

R6

7 **a)** Which one of these is **objective** – just deals with the facts and what happens?

b) Which one takes a definite **point of view**?

c) What is the point of view taken by the reviewer? Is it **good or bad**? How do you know?

113

Key Writing

Here are some key facts about the film *Billy Elliot*, which was mentioned at the start of this unit.

- It's about a boy from Newcastle who wants to be a ballet dancer.
- He decides to dance rather than box.
- Dad and brother are miners. They are on strike.
- Family doesn't have much money.
- Billy is taught by Mrs Wilkinson.
- Goes to London for an audition.

8 **a)** **Write one paragraph** about the film which just mentions the **facts** about the story and characters. You could start like this:

'The film is about...'

b) Now **write a second paragraph** in which you add some **personal opinions** or comments (good or bad) about the characters or story. For example, you could start:

- 'Billy seems to me...'
- 'I find the story is...'

④ Unit 5 Assignment: Drama reviewer

Assessment Focus

▶ **AF2** Produce texts which are appropriate to task, reader and purpose

---

You: write reviews and previews for the local newspaper of plays, musicals, shows (i.e. comedians, magicians, etc.), gigs/concerts (pop/rock bands, singers) and drama within local schools.

Your task: to write a preview of a piece of drama or a show that you have seen before it is shown publicly. Ideally, this should be for a real show or drama, but you can make it up if you wish. You will need to use a range of writing skills to inform the reader, and give your views about what you have seen.

Stage 1

Make notes about the performance. Use a table like the one below to help you. (The first few rows have been filled in as an example.)

Name or description of the show or performance.	West Side Story
When and where is it on?	15th–19th November, 7.30pm Ridgeway High School
Who is in it?	Simon Larwood as Tony; Lia Iqbal as Maria.
What happens? (The main story/facts.)	A boy and girl from opposing gangs in New York fall in love and...
Words that show your opinion of the performance and the people in it. (Pack in as much detail as possible using adverb + adjective phrases.)	
A statement summing up what you thought of it overall.	

Stage 2

Now take the content of your table and **plan your paragraphs**. Decide what you will put in each paragraph, using this writing plan. (Note: do not write them at this stage.)

Paragraph 1:
A general introduction about the performance saying who is putting it on, where and when it's on, and something about how good or bad it is.

Paragraph 2:
A brief summary of the events and characters.

Paragraph 3:

Final paragraph:

Stage 3

Write paragraph 1. Start by making a **general comment** or statement, such as:

> Ridgeway High School's production of *West Side Story*, which can be seen at the school every day this week, is terrifically good...

Use the present tense

Remember to use adverb + adjective phrases like this to pack in detail and express your opinion

Now **write the remaining three paragraphs**.

● Make sure each paragraph is separate.

● Make sure each character or performance is summed up.

● Add your opinion by using short words or phrases (for example, '*incredibly powerful*') and longer statements (for example, '*You should see this great performance by...*').

Challenge

Write a review about your own performance in a play, concert or group work in class.

● Write it mostly in the past tense.

● Include basic information about the performance.

● Give your opinion, looking back at what you did objectively and analysing its good and bad points.

Unit 6 Refugees

① Refugee Boy

Aims

▶ Read an extract from a narrative text
▶ Develop the skill of looking for key ideas
▶ Look at the way an author uses patterns to establish ideas (R5)
▶ Write your own introduction to a story

The following text is from the opening of a novel called _Refugee Boy_ by Benjamin Zephaniah.

Chapter 1
Ethiopia

As the family lay sleeping, soldiers kicked down the door of the house and entered, waving their rifles around erratically and shouting at the top of their voices. Alem ran into the room where his parents were, to find that they had been dragged out of bed dressed only in their nightclothes,
5 and forced to stand facing the wall.

The soldier who was in command went and stood so that his mouth was six inches away from Alem's father's ear and shouted, "What kind of man are you?"

Alem's father shuddered with fear; his voice trembled as he replied, "I
10 am an African."

Alem looked on terrified as the soldier shot a number of bullets into the floor around the feet of his father and mother.

His mother screamed with fear. "Please leave us! We only want peace."

The soldier continued shouting. "Are you Ethiopian or Eritrean? Tell
15 us, we want to know."

"I am an African," Alem's father replied.

The soldier raised his rifle and pointed it at Alem's father. "You are a traitor." He turned and pointed the rifle at Alem's mother. "And she is the enemy." Then he turned and pointed the rifle at Alem's forehead.

20 "And he is a mongrel."

Turning back to Alem's father, he dropped his voice and said, "Leave Ethiopia or die."

Chapter 2
Eritrea

As the family lay sleeping, soldiers kicked down the door of the house and entered, waving their rifles around erratically and shouting at the top

25 of their voices. Alem ran into the room where his parents were, to find that they had been dragged out of bed dressed only in their nightclothes, and forced to stand facing the wall.

The soldier who was in command went and stood so that his mouth was six inches away from Alem's mother's ear and shouted, "What kind

30 of woman are you?"

Alem's mother shuddered with fear; her voice trembled as she replied, "I am an African."

Alem looked on terrified as the soldier shot a number of bullets into the floor around the feet of his mother and father.

35 His father screamed with fear. "Please leave us! We only want peace."

The soldier continued shouting. "Are you Eritrean or Ethiopian? Tell us, we want to know."

"I am an African," Alem's mother replied.

The soldier raised his rifle and pointed it at Alem's mother. "You are a

40 traitor." He turned and pointed the rifle at Alem's father. "And he is the enemy." Then he turned and pointed the rifle at Alem's forehead. "And he is a mongrel."

Turning back to Alem's mother, he dropped his voice and said, "Leave Eritrea or die."

Ethiopia a country in North East Africa, on the Red Sea

Eritrea a country in North East Africa, on the Red Sea. It became part of Ethiopia in 1952 but a war of independence was fought from 1961 until 1993

erratically in an unpredictable way

mongrel an insulting name for someone of mixed parentage; it is usually used to describe animals

Key Reading

Narrative texts

This is a **narrative** text.

The main features of this text are:

● It has a structure that includes an opening (**introduction**), a problem (**complication**), a dramatic moment or event when everything comes to a head (**crisis**) and an ending (**resolution**) when things are sorted out. Since this is the beginning of a novel, only the introduction and problem are present. However, we can predict the possible crisis and ending from the title of the novel – *Refugee Boy.*

● It has **characters** who the story is about. We often hear their words (in direct speech) and thoughts.

● There is also a **narrator**, who tells the story in either the first person (I/we) or the third person (he/she/it), for example, 'as *he* replied, "I am an African."'

● It uses **powerful words**. The language of the narrative must be interesting to read or listen to, for example, 'Alem's mother *shuddered* with fear'.

1 Where is the problem or **complication introduced** in each chapter?

2 The story is written by an 'all-knowing' narrator.

  a) Which of the **three main characters** does it focus on?

  b) How can you tell this?

3 Find a piece of **direct speech** in Chapter 1.

4 The word 'turned' or 'turning' is used three times in the last two paragraphs of both chapters. What does this show about the way the commanding officer is **moving**?

Purpose

5 Below are three purposes of the opening of a novel. Which is the **main purpose** of this opening?

● To provide a **dramatic opening** to the story.

● To introduce the **main characters.**

● To make the reader want to know what **happens next**.

Point to the evidence in the text to support your choice.

Reading for meaning

6 **a)** Where does Chapter 1 take place? What **nationality** is Alem's **father**?

b) Where does Chapter 2 take place? What **nationality** is Alem's **mother**?

7 What must have **happened** to the family between Chapter 1 and Chapter 2?

8 Briefly **summarise the three or four differences** between Chapters 1 and 2, using a table like the one below.

Chapter 1	Chapter 2
Takes place in…	Takes place in…
Person attacked is…	Person attacked is…

9 Why do you think the writer has made these two chapters so **similar**? Write a sentence to explain what **effect** this has.

You could begin like this:
'By making the opening chapters so similar, the writer shows us…'

· ·

Focus on: Patterns of language

The writer of this text has selected his words very carefully to make a point about the way human beings behave. One way he has done this is through repetition of ideas and words or phrases. The most important example of this is his use of the same events and same characters in both chapters.

R5 **10** Find more **examples of repetition** within Chapter 1, where the author uses the same or similar words. Make a list like the one below and try to think of a reason for each use of repetition.

Repeated word or phrase	Reason
rifle	Keeps the idea of a powerful weapon in the reader's mind

A second pattern in this text is its use of words that describe the way people speak.

11 a) In pairs, list all the words that describe the way characters **speak**. For example, 'shouted' in paragraph 2.

  b) **Underline the words** used for the way the soldiers speak. What differences are there between these words and the words used for the way Alem's mother and father speak?

When a writer establishes a pattern, any break in that pattern is especially noticeable.

12 What is the **effect** of the soldier lowering his voice at the end of each chapter?

Key Writing

This extract is told by a **third-person** narrator who is outside the story. This is a good way to tell a complicated story as it means many different points of view can be presented.

Another way of telling the story would have been to use a **first-person** narrator. First-person narrative has a single point of view, usually that of one of the characters.

13 In pairs, discuss whether a **first- or third-person narrator is best** for a complex story with strong emotions such as Alem's.

S&L12

14 **Rewrite part of Chapter 1** (lines 1–16) from Alem's point of view, using first-person narrative. You will need to think about:
- what he saw and heard
- how he felt about the treatment of his parents
- his worst fear.

Remember to:
- use '**I**' for the narrator of the story (Alem)
- include a few extra details about how Alem reacts/feels, using **powerful language**.

You could start:

'I was sleeping peacefully one night when…'

Refugees and asylum seekers in the UK

Aims

▶ Read an information text

▶ Examine methods of presentation

▶ Examine the way webpages are organised (R8)

▶ Give a presentation (S&L3)

The following extract is from the Commission for Racial Equality's website.

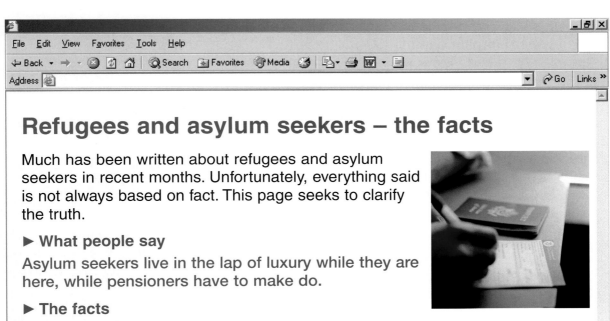

Refugees and asylum seekers – the facts

Much has been written about refugees and asylum seekers in recent months. Unfortunately, everything said is not always based on fact. This page seeks to clarify the truth.

► What people say

5   Asylum seekers live in the lap of luxury while they are here, while pensioners have to make do.

► The facts

In 2003, a single pensioner gets a guaranteed minimum income of
10   £98.15 a week. A single asylum seeker gets less than half of that – only £37.77 a week – 30% below the poverty line.

Asylum seekers are not allowed to claim welfare benefits. If they are destitute, all they can do is to apply for help to the National Asylum Support Service (NASS), the government department responsible for supporting destitute
15   asylum applicants. There is no question of an asylum seeker being able to choose where they live, and the accommodation is nearly always in hard-to-let areas where few people want to live. NASS does not give either asylum seekers or landlords any money for luxury items or furnishings.

▶ What people say

20 Refugees and Asylum Seekers increase unemployment and take jobs away from the host population.

▶ The facts

There is no evidence that refugees and asylum seekers take jobs away from the host population.

25 Asylum Seekers are not permitted to work despite evidence that they would prefer to support themselves than rely on the State. On getting status refugees pay taxes and generally contribute as others do. Higher proportions of foreign-born workers, including refugees, work in construction, cleaning, agriculture and manufacturing than native workers, reflecting the contribution they make to the

30 less popular industries. There is also reliance on migrants to fill the gaps present in the UK labour market: according to the Greater London Authority, 23% of doctors and 47% of nurses working within the NHS were born outside the UK.

The UK's working population is declining. The UN's Population Division reports that low birth rates mean the EU will need to import 1.6 million migrants a

35 year simply to keep its working-age population stable between now and 2050.

▶ What people say

Asylum seekers are just a huge expense to the British taxpayer.

▶ The facts

A recent Home Office study found that, far from being a burden on UK taxpayers,

40 migrants made a net contribution of approximately £2.5 billion to income tax in 1999–2000. Throughout history, migrants (including refugees) have made invaluable contributions to our economic and cultural life, for example:

- ▶ fish and chips were brought to the UK by 17th-century Jews expelled from Portugal;

45 - ▶ Alec Issigonis, who fled the war between Turkey and Greece, was the brain behind the Mini and the Morris Minor;

- ▶ Karl Marx and Sigmund Freud were refugees; and

- ▶ Sir John Hoblon, the first Governor of the Bank of England, was the grandson of an asylum seeker from France.

---

asylum seeker a person asking to be allowed to stay in another country

refugee a person who has been forced to leave their country because it is not safe for them to stay

poverty line people who live below the poverty line suffer hardship through lack of money

destitute completely without money

host population the people of the country where asylum is applied for

status officially recognised as refugees

proportions part of the total number

migrants people moving from one country to another

labour market total of jobs to be filled

net contribution added overall

Key Reading

Information texts

This text is an **information** text. Its **purpose** is to give clear information about a topic.

The main features of this text are:

● It consists of an **introductory statement** followed by **logically ordered sections**. For example, Introduction – 'Much has been written about refugees and asylum seekers in recent months'.

● Verbs are in the **present tense**. For example, 'Asylum seekers *are* not allowed to claim welfare benefits'

● **Headings** and **subheadings** make it easier to find information, for example, 'What people say'.

● Both **general information** and **specific facts**, often using **technical language**, are included, for example, 'Karl Marx and Sigmund Freud were refugees' and 'migrants made a *net contribution* of approximately £2.5 billion'.

1 After the introduction, each of the three sections is organised in the same way. Describe how each section is **organised**.

2 Most of the text is in the present tense. Which section is in the **past tense**?

3 a) Explain each of these **technical terms**:

  ● guaranteed minimum income
  ● construction industry
  ● native population.

b) What is the **effect** of using technical terms in this information text?

Purpose

4 In pairs, discuss whether you think the **main purpose** of this text is:

- to inform people about asylum seekers
- to correct some people's ideas about asylum seekers
- to start a debate about asylum seekers.

5 Why do you think the Commission for Racial Equality (CRE) decided that a webpage giving this information was necessary?

Reading for meaning

6 a) The webpage is packed with facts. Look again at each of the three main sections and **write down the comment each section begins with** in a table like the one below.

b) Then find at least **three specific facts** in each section that give information on the comment. Add these in note form in your table.

Comment 1: Asylum seekers live in… luxury… here, while pensioners have to make do.	Comment 2:	Comment 3:
1. Single pensioner gets £98.15 a week; asylum seeker gets £37.77		
2.		

c) Be ready to **share your findings** with the class.

7 Look at the bullet points in section 3. What two things do the people listed here have **in common**?

Focus on: Organising information on a webpage

Scrolling versus turning

In a long paper-based text you get to the next piece of information by **turning** the page. In a long computer-based text you get to the next piece of information by **scrolling down** the screen using the mouse or an arrow key.

8 a) How do **paper-based texts** help the reader to **navigate** around the whole text? Think of three features.

b) How does the reader get to the information they need quickly?

R8

9 a) How do **computer-based texts** help the reader to **navigate** around the whole site or document? Think of two features. Refer back to the website on page 125–126, if necessary.

b) How does the reader get to the information they need quickly?

Design layout

The Commission for Racial Equality (CRE) text is from a webpage and is designed to give people information quickly and easily.

10 In pairs, discuss the **design features** of the page that make it easy for readers to find information. You might consider:

- repeated features
- use of bold type
- use of numbers or percentages.
- font size
- bullet points

11 With your partner, decide which of the above design features could be used to present or highlight this type of information more clearly.

Key Speaking and Listening

S&L3 **12** The CRE information is designed as a webpage. You are going to use the same information to **produce a formal presentation** for your class on how refugees live in the UK and what they have achieved.

a) In pairs, work through the information in your tables from question 6. **Select** which pieces of **information** from each of the three sections you will include in your five minute presentation.

b) Next decide **who will present** each of the sections.

c) Plan your **visual aids**, for example, prepare a bar chart of information about incomes or write key figures for display on an OHT. Write key points on prompt cards to remind you what to say next.

d) Rehearse your presentation to ensure the links between sections are smooth. Try to vary your pace so that the information remains clear and interesting for your audience. Be ready to make your presentation.

Remember to:

- Use the present tense mostly, but the past tense when referring to past events.

- Move from each general point to a specific example.

- Include necessary technical terms but always explain them the first time they are used.

③ Student action

Aims

▶ Read an advice text

▶ Think about audiences for texts

▶ Look at how advice texts are organised

▶ Explore different degrees of formality in written texts

▶ Practise writing an advice text

The following text is from a leaflet aimed at students who are concerned about the treatment of asylum seekers in the UK.

STAR

(Student Action for Refugees)

Refugee Policy is PANTS campaign
Campaign Action 5: Section 55
Write to/Visit your local MP

Students are especially well placed to lobby those in positions of influence because you are new voters with whom politicians want to engage and you have a strong collective voice. Writing a letter to or meeting your MP is a simple and effective way of campaigning; it is your chance to inform your MP of the issues and it adds to the voice for refugees.

It is your right as a voter to let your local MP know about issues of concern to you and your local community. It is also part of your MP's job to read and reply to letters from constituents.

Having been involved in STAR and having volunteered with local refugee agencies/ projects **you are likely to be more informed about refugee and asylum issues than your local MP**. MPs are expected to answer questions from constituents on a diverse range of subjects, so won't have in-depth knowledge of many issues. You will be able to give them the facts and tell them the reality from your experiences!

You can also ask your MP to raise your concerns with the Home Secretary, who is obliged to respond. If a significant number of MPs ask questions on a particular issue then the Home Secretary is forced to take action.

To find out who your local MP is, call the House of Commons Information Office 020 7219 4272.

You might also be able to get hold of your MP at their constituency office. You should be able to find out the phone number at a local library or town hall or by searching under their name on the Internet.

5

10

15

20

25

30

35

40

131

Visit your MP...

At Westminster – You can arrange to visit your MP in the Central Lobby in parliament, when the House of Commons is sitting. You will need to make an
45 appointment to see them, to check they're going to be around. NB You need special permission to organise a mass lobby.

In their constituency – MPs also hold regular 'surgeries' in their constituencies
50 (find out the details from their office), and groups such as STAR often visit their local MPs. Take along three/four people and decide who will speak about which issue. Be clear about what you would like to get
55 from the meeting: request a parliamentary question on Section 55 or the MP's support for STAR's campaign. Ask them for their personal opinion about the issue and be polite and concise in stating
60 your concerns.

Invite your MP to visit campus

Why not go one step further and ask for your MP to be a speaker at one of your STAR meetings. Use the Campaign Action on Section 55 as a
65 reason to invite them and take the opportunity to advertise the meeting well to get lots of students along to ask questions. You could also arrange a photo opportunity as
70 an added incentive for your MP to attend, and get some coverage in the student press.

● Don't forget to give them a STAR leaflet and the Campaign briefing.

Section 55 a government ruling which takes away National Asylum Support Service support from asylum applicants who do not apply for asylum as soon as they reach the UK

pants (slang) very bad

campus the site of a university

lobby try and influence a member of parliament

positions of influence having political power

issues of concern things that are worrying

constituents the people who live in the area that elects an MP

obliged have no choice

surgeries times when an MP is available for meetings with his or her constituents

photo opportunity a chance for newspapers to take a photograph

Key Reading

Advice texts

This is an **advice** text. Its **purpose** is to advise the reader to do (or not to do) something.

The main features of this text are:

- It has a **series of points** in a **logical order**, for example, 'Invite your MP to visit campus'.

- It uses **direct address** using some **imperatives** or the words 'you' or 'your', for example, '*Be* clear about what *you* would like to get from the meeting'

- It uses **formal language** but an **informal tone** where suited to the audience, for example, 'Refugee Policy is PANTS'.

- It has a **design layout** which helps to make the structure of the advice clear, for example, subheadings to show sections of advice.

1 The campaigners decided to use the slang term 'pants' as the title of their campaign. How would this appeal to their student **audience**?

2 Look closely at the use of direct address in section 1, 'Write to/Visit your local MP'. What **effect** does the constant use of 'you' and 'your' have on the reader?

3 **a)** What **three pieces of advice** are given in paragraph 2, section 2, 'Visit your MP...'?

b) Find the **three imperative verbs** that signal this.

Grammar for reading

Imperative verbs **tell** (or **command**) you directly to do something, for example: '*Write* to your MP as soon as you can'.

In advice texts, imperatives are often 'softened' by adding phrases like '*Try to* write to your MP as soon as you can.'

---

4 What is the purpose of the **bullet point** right at the end of the leaflet?

• •

Purpose

The purpose of this advice text is to help students in Higher Education campaign on the issue of refugees.

5 **a)** In pairs, discuss how the **organisation** of the text makes the advice clear and interesting. Think about its use of:

● headings and subheadings

● bold text.

b) **Make a list of the subheadings** and summarise in one sentence the **main point of advice being given** in each, for example:

> Write to/Visit your local MP: main point — writing a letter to or meeting your MP is a simple and effective way of campaigning.

Reading for meaning

Advice texts not only give clear pieces of advice, they also back them up with good **reasons** for taking the advice. For example, in section 1 a number of reasons are put forward for why writing to an MP will be effective.

> 1. Students are new voters so MPs will listen to them.
>
> 2. As constituents, they have the right to talk to their MP.
>
> 3.

6 What is the **third reason** given to support this piece of advice?

The main points in an advice text can also be backed up by **examples** or by **expanding** the main point. This technique is used later in the leaflet. For example, in section 2, under the subheading 'At Westminster' the main point is expanded like this:

1. Be sure to make an appointment to see your MP.

2. Seek special permission for a mass lobby.

7 Look again at the last piece of advice under the subheading 'Invite your MP to visit campus'. Note down the **two points** that expand this advice.

Focus on: Formal language, informal tone

The advice in this text is on a serious matter and introduces some complicated ideas. The writer has therefore chosen **formal language** to match his topic. For example, this sentence uses formal language to put across an idea about the way a political process works:

> <u>If</u> a significant number of MPs ask questions on a particular issue, <u>then</u> the Home Secretary is forced to take action.

It uses a **conditional sentence** structure to do this.

Grammar for reading

Conditional sentences usually have two parts or clauses. In the first, a condition is set by the connective 'if'. In the second, the result of completing the condition is stated, often using the connective 'then'.

Contracted words or phrases show where a letter has been missed out by an apostrophe, for example: 'don't' instead of 'do not'. In writing they create an informal effect.

S7

8 Read the following pairs of sentences. Then **rewrite them** as one longer conditional sentence using 'if' and 'then'.

- Arrange a photo opportunity on campus.
- It is much more likely that your MP will attend.

- Seek special permission from your MP.
- You will be able to hold a mass lobby.

9 In pairs, look through the text to **find examples of these features**:

- informal words or phrases
- contracted words or phrases
- direct address
- punctuation for humorous effect.

Be ready to share your findings.

Key Writing

Wr15 **10** The STAR campaign manager has asked you to **produce a poster** based on the advice in the leaflet. The aim is to pass on the key points to students and encourage them to contact their MPs.

a) Reread your list of main points and reasons or expanded points from questions 5, 6 and 7. Then choose the **four points** you will use for the poster. Arrange them in the most effective order.

b) Find or draw **one image** that will help give your advice impact.

c) Decide on a **heading** for your poster, using the campaign name.

d) Write out your four points.
Remember to:

- use imperatives to tell the reader the main point
- use some informal language to appeal to the reader
- highlight key words using bold or underlining.

④ Unit 6 Assignment: How to write to an MP

Assessment Focus

▶ AF2 Produce texts which are appropriate to task, reader and purpose

> **You:** are a campaign organiser.
>
> **Your task:** to design a leaflet advising students how to write a letter to their MP.

Stage 1

Begin by **planning the different sections** of your leaflet. Here are some section headings. Select the four most important headings for your purpose.

- Advice on how to find out who your MP is and how to contact him or her (take this from the STAR leaflet)
- Advice on formal letter layout
- Advice on getting involved with other STAR campaigns
- Advice on the content of the letter
- Encouragement to write the letter as soon as possible
- Details of the next STAR meeting.

Decide in which order to place your four sections.

Stage 2

Draft your first section – try to give general advice on the purpose of the leaflet and how to get in touch with the MP.

Next, introduce how to lay out a formal letter. Decide how you will **present the diagram** on page 140 in your leaflet.

● Will you add notes around the edge to show the purpose of each feature?

● Will you include a paragraph or bullet points above the diagram?

Think about how you will present advice on the content of the four paragraphs in the letter. Here are points you need to include:

● the **introduction** and what should be said in it

● suggestions about the **points to make** in the second and third paragraphs

● suggestions for the **examples** in paragraphs 2 and 3 – you can use the information in texts 1 and 2 in this unit for ideas about this

● advice about how to **conclude** the letter.

Finally, decide how you will round off the leaflet. What are the key points you will remind students about? Complete your **first draft**.

MP's address		Your address
		Date

Dear *Name*

Introductory paragraph

Paragraph 2 – point with examples

Paragraph 3 – point with examples

Final paragraph – what action you would like the MP to take

Yours faithfully

Signature

Your name

Stage 3

Look back over your draft to see if you can **improve it**.

Remember to:

● use imperative verbs for the main advice points

● include a reason or expand on each piece of advice

● use direct address

● make the tone informal in places to keep the readers' interest, for example, contracted words, informal words/phrases.

Challenge

Although it is good to include some informal language for your student audience, it also helps to use formal language to make a key point. Try using a phrase like 'It is…' or 'There are…' to create this effect.

For example,
'*It is* important that you use the correct layout for a formal letter when writing to your MP.'

This sounds more formal and distanced than:
'Use the correct layout for a formal letter…'

Unit 7 New media

① The Birth of The Bug

Aims

▶ Read an advert for a digital radio, and explore how it adapts its language to suit a particular audience and purpose (S9)

▶ Analyse the underlying meaning of a cartoon strip

▶ Think about how texts are shaped by the technology they use (R9)

▶ Give a presentation in a persuasive way (S&L4)

The following text is an advert in a gadget magazine.

The Bug is one seriously cool collaboration between yours truly, Wayne Hemingway of hEMINGWAYdESIGN, and PURE Digital. It doesn't look like a normal radio, because it isn't a normal radio! It's DAB digital radio, so that means it's got a huge display to tell you the name of the DJ or the track you're listening to or just the time if that's all you're after. It's got things that are cooler than a penguin in a snowstorm, like being able to pause the radio to answer your mobile, or even rewind to the start of a track and then record it to SD card. So you can enjoy it over and over until you're sick of it! And then there's all the fabulous stations you can only get on digital radio, like XFM, Smash Hits, 1Xtra, Core, Galaxy, YAAR – you name it! Anyway, enough of me rambling, have a read, and Get The Bug.

Wayne Hemingway

Six months later....

Wayne's toils pay off...

THE BUG IS BORN

Following the runaway success of The Bug...

Dab Hand

Wayne is "offered" his next assignment.

THE END.....?

collaboration a product developed by more than one person or business

toils efforts, hard work

assignment project, job

Key Reading

Persuasion texts

This text is a **persuasion** text. Its **purpose** is to persuade the reader to buy The Bug digital radio.

The main features of this text are:

- It has a **series of points** supporting a **single viewpoint**, for example, '*And then there's all the fabulous stations you can only get on digital radio…*'.

- It has **visual images** to grab the interest of the audience, for example, *the cartoon strip*.

- It uses **emotive and colourful language**, for example, '*It's got things that are cooler than a penguin in a snowstorm…*'

- It uses **direct address** to gain the attention of the audience and win them over, for example, '*So you can enjoy it over and over…*'.

1 What **point** does the advert make at the beginning of the text on page 143?

2 There are two different styles of **visual image** used in this advert. What are they?

3 'Anyway, enough of me rambling.'
Is this phrase intended to **make the reader feel**:

- **irritated** that Hemingway is rambling

- **comfortable** reading his words

- ready to **read on**?

4 Wayne Hemingway **addresses the audience directly** in the cartoon as well. Where?

. . . .

Purpose

 5 What is the **main purpose** of the cartoon in this text? Is it:

- to recount a true story of how The Bug was designed
- to attract attention by putting something unusual in an advert
- to entertain the audience by telling a fun story
- to tell you more about the designer of The Bug?

Discuss these options in small groups and come to an agreement, if you can. (Is more than one of them true of the text?)

6 The main text on page 143 tries to persuade the reader to buy The Bug. It does this by making points about how good it is. **Note down two points** that it makes.

. . . .

Reading for meaning

The cartoon strip on pages 142–143 can be 'read' in many different ways. One 'reading' is that it is simply telling a story.

7 **Rewrite the story** in a single paragraph. You may want to begin like this:

> Wayne Hemmingway, the famous designer, was buying a Mars Bar and chips at his favourite chippy one day...

The cartoon can also be 'read' as another way of selling the product. For example:

Suggests he is famous, like a film star

Suggests The Bug is so amazing that people will want to know how it was ever invented

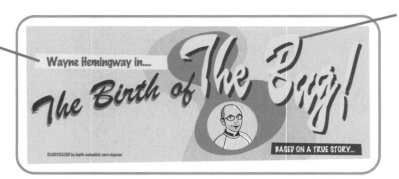

8 In pairs, continue 'reading' the cartoon as a way of selling the product. **Make notes** on each frame, as shown above. Think about what the cartoon is telling you about:

● the **product** (for example, its quality and style)

● the **designer**.

9 The cartoon also forms part of The Bug's website. What **differences** do you think there are in the web version? What **features** could make this text longer, louder and more interesting on the Internet?

R9

· ·

Focus on: Suiting audience and purpose

The Bug advert is written for a particular audience and purpose:

● **audience** – young men and women who like gadgets and style

● **purpose** – to persuade these people to buy The Bug.

The language of the text at the top of page 143 is carefully geared to this audience and purpose. For example:

Informal language – colloquialism
Tone – cool and trendy
Emotive words – makes you think 'style'

Informal language – colloquialism

> The Bug is one seriously cool collaboration between yours truly, Wayne Hemingway of hEMINGWAYdESIGN, and PURE Digital. It doesn't look like a normal radio, because it isn't a normal radio!

Informal language – contraction

Tone – humorous

Emotive punctuation – exclamation mark

10 In pairs, find **one example** of each of the **four features** below. Each example should show how the chosen language is suited to its audience and purpose.

S9

- **Informal language** – colloquialisms, contractions
- **Emotive language** – words or punctuation to make you feel a certain way
- **Tone** – cool, funny or friendly
- **Direct address** – makes the text personal to you.

Grammar for reading

Colloquialisms are words or phrases that are more suitable in spoken than in written language. For example: '*He had a seriously cool haircut.*'

Key Speaking and Listening

11 You and your partner are top advertising executives. You have been hired by Wayne Hemingway and PURE Digital to come up with a great advertising campaign for The Bug.

You dream up the cartoon strip 'The Birth of The Bug'. Now you have to **persuade your clients that the cartoon is a great idea**. You are going to do this in a spoken commentary.

a) Look back over your work on questions 7, 8 and 9. **Use the notes** you made then, and add any good points made in class discussion.

b) Then decide how you are going to **divide up** the presentation. Here a couple of possibilities:

● One of you tells the 'straight' story while the other gives the underlying meaning

● One focuses on the words and the other on the images.

c) Finally, think what particular techniques you can use to persuade your audience. Use an appropriate **tone** and **emotive language** to win them over.

d) **Practise** your presentation until you are happy with it. Be ready to present the cartoon strip.

The Internet – a waste of time?

▶ Read a newspaper article that expresses a point of view about the Internet

▶ Explore how texts like this signpost which way the argument is going (Wr14)

▶ Think about how and why irony is used in a text (R7)

The following text is an article from *The Independent*.

Don't believe the hype: the Internet's a waste of time

This week, plans for a new Internet university were announced. This is the latest headline in a long list of wonderful things that a computer and modem can do. There are e-bookshops where you can buy self-help guides to help you deal with the anxiety you felt ever since you divulged your

credit card number over the Internet. There are virtual jobs in virtual offices where you go virtually mad never talking to another human being from one day to the next.

Suddenly the Internet is the solution to everything. The Prime Minister is lying awake at night trying to think of a way forward for the troubled peace process in Northern Ireland. "Have you thought about looking on the Internet?" says Cherie. And there it is, instantly available – and all for the price of a local phone call. The

20 way to end world poverty, the secret of eternal happiness, the cure for cancer… apparently you can find out something about almost anything by logging on to the Internet.

The only problem is that when you enter the words "cure" and "cancer", your search engine will find four million sites, the first of
25 which is the diary of a 15-year-old boy from Milwaukee whose favourite band is the Cure and whose star sign is Cancer. And for some reason you find yourself reading ten pages about his trip to summer camp in Vermont before you accept that this site isn't going to have the information you were looking for.

30 The usefulness of the Internet has been hyped out of all proportion. All it does is make information more easily available. The downside of this is that in doing so it creates an enormous amount of new material, most of which is just information for its own sake. Like mobile phone users on trains on the way to the
35 office, loudly reporting that they are on a train and on their way into the office, much of what is posted on the Internet is up there because it can be, not because it needs to be.

Today libraries are closing while funding for the Internet seems limitless. Is this because we have read all the books there are to
40 read? No, it is simply that the Internet is new. It is so new that even the cynical British have failed to see that it is not a super-highway at all, but the information equivalent of the M25 in the rush hour.

divulged revealed
limitless endless
cynical suspicious

Key Reading

Argument texts

This is an **argument** text. Its **purpose** is to express a point of view, and persuade the reader to agree with it.

The main features of this text are:

- It makes a **series of points** in a **logical order**, for example, t*he first paragraph makes the point that computers can do lots of 'wonderful things'.*

- The main points are backed up by **evidence** or **reasons**, for example, *'and for some reason you find yourself reading ten pages…'*

- It uses **formal** but **effective** language, for example, *'today libraries are closing while funding for the Internet seems limitless…'*

- It uses clear **signposting** of the argument to make the logic clear, for example, *'The only problem is that…'*

1 Summarise the **author's point of view** in one sentence.

2 What **point** does the author make in paragraph 2? What **evidence** does he give?

3 The author calls the Internet the 'information equivalent of the M25 in the rush hour' (line 42). What makes this image **effective**?

4 The phrase 'The only problem is' (line 23) signposts that the author is about to make an objection to a statement.

a) What is the **statement**?

b) What is the **objection**?

Purpose

The purpose of an argument text is to put forward your point of view. An effective argument is made up of several points. Each point is a step in the argument.

The author of this article begins by seeming to make some points *in favour of* the Internet. These are:

● Computers help us do lots of wonderful things (paragraph 1)

● The Internet is the solution to everything (paragraph 2).

5 In the rest of the article he makes three points *against* the Internet.

a) Working with a partner, **discuss** what these points are.

b) Write down a **one-sentence summary** of each point.

Reading for meaning

Sometimes you think a sentence means one thing, then you realise it means the exact opposite! This happens in the first two paragraphs of the newspaper article. For example:

The **explicit** meaning is, 'Here is another example of the many wonderful things available on the Internet.'

There are e-bookshops where you can buy self-help guides to help you deal with the anxiety you felt ever since you divulged your credit card number over the Internet.

The **implied** meaning is, 'e-bookshops aren't useful at all. The Internet only causes problems.'

This is an example of **irony**. It can be a powerful weapon in an argument.

Grammar for reading

Implied meaning is what a text suggests, but doesn't actually say. For example: '*It's maths, my favourite lesson,*' he groaned. This implies that he does not enjoy maths.

Explicit or **literal meaning** is the surface or 'obvious' meaning of a text.

Irony is when words are used to imply the opposite of what they normally mean.

6 In pairs, **draw up a table** like the one below. Find at least two more examples of **irony** in paragraphs 1 and 2 of the article. Write down the explicit and the implied meaning in each case.

Sentence	Explicit meaning	Implied meaning
'This is the latest headline in a long list of wonderful things…'	The Internet can do lots of wonderful things	They aren't that wonderful at all
'There are e-bookshops where you can buy…'	You can even buy books on the Internet	But only to help you with the problems that the Internet causes
'There are virtual jobs in virtual offices…'	You can work from home just using the Internet	

Focus on: Signposting arguments

Arguments are more effective when they make it clear which way they are going. Sentence signposts do this very well. In the newspaper article, for example:

> The usefulness of the Internet has been hyped out of all proportion. <u>All it does</u> is make information more easily available.

Reason given for the main point. The underlined part is a signpost telling you that 'making information available' doesn't count for very much

7 Look at the next sentence (line 32). It has a sentence signpost, 'The downside of this is…'. What does the signpost tell you immediately about **where the argument is going**?

Key Writing

> ● Using the Internet allows you to buy things without hitting the High Street.
>
> ● You can't see the quality of the things you buy.

Wr14 **8** **a) Rewrite the statements** above so that the argument is clear to the reader.

● You could use a simple connective, for example 'but' or 'however'.

● You could use a sentence signpost.

● You may want to keep the two sentences separate, or combine them as one.

b) In pairs, come up with three different ways to signpost this piece of argument.

3 Rags to riches

Aims

▶ Read a true rags-to-riches story

▶ Remind yourself how recount texts are written

▶ Investigate how to combine clauses to make your sentences more effective (S1)

The following text comes from *The Scotsman*.

How to make a mobile for-tune

If there is one man who knows just how big ringtones have become then it's Alexander Amosu. The 28-year-old is the man behind the UK's number one provider of phone tunes.

And it's a real rags-to-riches tale. He was born in Britain, but moved to Nigeria at the age of two with his parents. Ten years later, he returned to Britain to live with his grandmother and younger brother.

They moved into a council house in north London and there was so little room, he had to sleep on the sofa in the sitting room. At school, he couldn't relate to the other children who wore Nike and Adidas trainers. He didn't even have enough money for school dinners. "All the kids that everyone liked had the latest gear," he says. "I couldn't fit in. I had really geeky and ugly clothes. I had two options – I could either go in just these trainers or I could work for them."

He got a paper round and bought himself a pair of Nike trainers. His classmates suddenly started talking to him. "From there I thought if I needed something I would just have to work hard for it. I saved the money and kitted myself out to look pretty and before you knew it I was quite popular in school," he says.

While at college he put on parties and set up a house-cleaning business which eventually made more than £1500 a week.

Then, in 2000, when he was just 24, he sent his brother a ringtone he had made on a phone with a composing facility. The tune was Big Pimpin' by Jay-Z, and he had painstakingly keyed in the notes on the phone's keypad.

His brother's phone went off at college and immediately all his friends wanted it. Alexander made them pay £1 for the ringtone. In the first day he made £7. "I thought, this is fantastic! What would happen if I made a catalogue of ringtones and advertised it?" he says. He did some research and found only one company in the UK and several in Germany providing ringtones.

He decided to specialise in R'n'B music and, within six weeks, had come up with a further six ringtones. He installed an extra phone line, with a premium-rate number charging £1.50 a minute, in the council house he was living in with his parents. He advertised the number on the back of 20,000 fliers he made for his next party. On the first day, R'n'B Ringtones made £97. He gave up university.

Within four months he moved the firm into offices in Islington and employed 21 staff, selling 1000 ringtones. "We were making the songs as they were coming out," he says. In the first year turnover was £1.2 million. In 2002, he was named Young Entrepreneur of the Year at the Institute of Directors Black Enterprise Awards.

He now lives in a three-storey townhouse and drives a Porsche. He has also bought homes in Alicante and Nigeria.

facility feature
painstakingly carefully and thoroughly
entrepreneur someone who uses skills and takes risks to set up a business

enterprise showing boldness and energy in the business world

Key Reading

Recount texts

This text is a **recount** or **chronological report**. Its **purpose** is to recount or tell the reader about a series of events.

The main features of this text are:

- It is told mainly in the **past tense**, for example, '*He was born in Britain*'.

- It describes events in **time order** and refers to time spans and shifts, for example, '*but moved to Nigeria at the age of two*'. This comes after the information that Alexander was born in Britain.

- It uses **time connectives**, for example, '*Ten years later*'.

1 Why is the newspaper interested in Alexander Amosu?

2 **a)** Where is the first **past tense verb** in the passage?

   b) What **tense** are the verbs up to this point?

3 **a)** What did Alexander do in **2000**?

   b) What happened to him in **2002**?

4 Identify three different **time connectives** used in this text.

Purpose

5 What do you think is the **main purpose** of this newspaper article?

● To give you advice on how to make a fortune.

● To show how working hard gets you rewards.

● To tell you how Amosu became the number one provider of phone tunes.

● To give you information about mobile ringtones.

Point to the evidence in the text that supports your answer.

Reading for meaning

This recount text is written mainly in time order. However, it begins in the present, then 'fast rewinds' to the beginning of Alexander's life. Recounts in newspapers often use time shifts like this.

6 Why is this an **effective technique** in recounts? Look at the newspaper stories below. They also begin in the present tense.

Use the 'fast rewind' technique to **write the next sentence** in each story.

> **Tornado strikes Norfolk**
> The people of Chatswell are waking up today to a scene of devastation.

> **Murderer released**
> Gerry Giles leaves Wandsworth Prison a free man today.

Make sure you have used the **past tense**.

7 **a)** Draw up a **timeline** of the events in this recount, like the one below. Start with Amosu's birth and include dates where you can.

b) Some events are described in greater detail. Indicate these using **branching lines** from the main notes on the timeline.

c) Why has the writer gone into such **detail** at these points in the story?

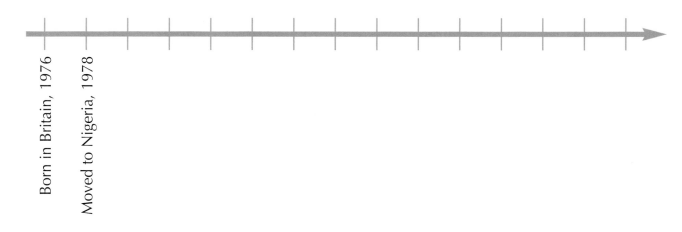

Born in Britain, 1976

Moved to Nigeria, 1978

'**Have**' is a very common verb, which is used in many different ways. Here are two:

● It can mean 'own' or 'experience', for example, '*I have two sisters.*' The past tense of 'have' is 'had', for example, '*He had a brand-new Ferrari.*'

● It can also mean 'must' when it is added to another verb, for example, '*I have to go*', and in the past tense, '*She had to stop.*'

8 **a)** Spot **five uses** of the verb 'have' in paragraphs 3 and 4 of the text. What is its meaning in each case?

b) What **tense** are they in?

Focus on: More effective sentences

Combining short sentences often makes writing more effective. For example, this is what the author of the recount writes in line 8:

> *He was born in Britain, but moved to Nigeria at the age of two with his parents.*

She could have written:

> *He was born in Britain. He moved to Nigeria at the age of two with his parents.*

Combining the two sentences has these advantages:.

● It is less repetitive ('He was born…';'He moved…').
● The connective ('but') shows how the two clauses are related.
● The new sentence sounds and looks better.

9 Look carefully at the next sentence:

> *Ten years later, he returned to Britain to live with his grandmother and younger brother.*

a) In pairs, discuss why this is better than using two separate sentences.

b) What **connective phrase** is used, and what does it do?

Key Writing

10 Here are some notes for a short magazine article about Dominic McVey (another young entrepreneur). Your task is to **write the article**.

> **Dominic McVey**
> Born 1985. At 13, imported motorised scooters from USA. Set up Scooters UK Ltd. Became millionaire at 14. Britain's youngest self-made millionaire.
> **Other business interests:** Manager of boy band *Most Wanted*. Has a web-design business. Wants to move into politics.

- Try to **combine clauses** to make longer sentences.
- Add **connectives** to show how the clauses relate to each other, for example, 'but', 'and', 'however', 'when', 'as', 'since'.

Make sure some of these are time connectives to show any time shifts in Dominic's story. You could begin like this:

> Dominic McVey was only 13 when he began importing motorised scooters from the USA.

> **Grammar for reading**
>
> A **clause** is a basic part of a sentence. It usually contains subject, verb and object. When you combine sentences, each becomes a clause.

④ Unit 7 Assignment: The Internet is cool

 ## Assessment Focus

▶ **AF3** Organise and present whole texts effectively, sequencing and structuring information, ideas and events

---

You: are writing a letter to the newspaper that printed John O'Farrell's article.

Your task: to put the case *for* the internet.

Stage 1

Brainstorm the reasons why the Internet is cool. You may want to reread the article on pages 149–150 by John O'Farrell. Can you think of your own arguments to undermine his points? **Draw up a spidergram**, like the one begun below.

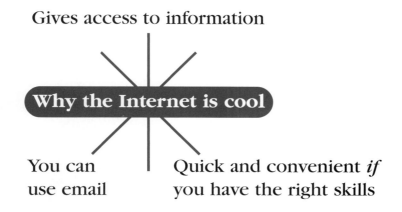

Gives access to information

Why the Internet is cool

You can use email

Quick and convenient *if* you have the right skills

Stage 2

Now **plan your letter**. Choose your three best points in favour of the Internet. Write down a brief **summary** of each one.

When drafting your letter, you will write a short paragraph on each of these main points.

● Decide on the best order for your paragraphs.

● Then jot down one or two reasons or evidence to back up each main point. These may include points against John O'Farrell's arguments.

Stage 3

Now **draft your paragraphs**. Remember to:

● lay it out like a letter to a newspaper

● use formal language

● signpost your argument, using connectives or sentence signposts, so that the reader knows which way it is going.

For example:

Main point, with signposting underlined

> One reason the Internet is cool is because you can use email.
> Email is great because it's so quick.

Reason given for
the main point

Read through your letter again. Can you make any words more powerful or interesting? Can you tighten up your style?

For example:

Signpost rephrased to make it snappier

> But the coolest thing about the Internet is email.
> Email beats snail mail hands down.

Reason is rephrased in
more colourful language

Challenge

Can you use **irony** to good effect in your letter?

How could you use it to:
- undermine John O'Farrell's arguments?
- create humour?

① "Gas! Gas!"

Aims

▶ Read an extract from a novel about the First World War

▶ Develop your understanding of how a writer uses imagery to make effective descriptions (W11)

▶ Write your own description, using these techniques (Wr5)

This is an extract from *Private Peaceful* by Michael Morpurgo, which is set in the First World War. It is told by a soldier, Thomas Peaceful.

I am writing to Mother – I haven't written for a while and I am feeling guilty about it. My pencil keeps breaking and I am sharpening it again. Everyone else is lying asleep in the sun or is sitting about smoking and
5   chatting. Nipper Martin is cleaning his rifle again. He's always very particular about that.

"Gas! Gas!"

The cry goes up and is echoed all along the trench. For a moment we are frozen with panic. We have
10   trained for this time and time again, but nonetheless we fumble clumsily, feverishly with our gas masks.

"Fix bayonets!" Hanley's yelling while we're still trying frantically to pull on our gas masks. We grab our rifles and fix bayonets. We're on the firestep looking
15   out into no-man's-land, and we see it rolling towards

us, this dreaded killer cloud we have heard so much about but have never seen for ourselves until now. Its deadly tendrils are searching ahead, feeling their way forward in long yellow wisps, scenting me, searching for me. Then finding me out,
20 the gas turns and drifts straight for me. I'm shouting inside my gas mask. "Christ! Christ!" Still the gas comes, wafting over our wire, through our wire, swallowing everything in its path.

The gas is only feet away now. In a moment it will be on
25 me, around me, in me. I crouch down hiding my face between my knees, praying it will float over my head, over the top of the trench and seek out someone else. But it does not. It's all around me. I tell myself I will not breathe, I must not breathe. Through a yellow mist I see the trench filling up with it. It
30 drifts into the dugouts, snaking into every nook and cranny, looking for me. It wants to seek us all out, to kill us all, every one of us. Still I do not breathe. I see men running, staggering, falling. I hear Pete shouting for me. Then he's grabbing me and we run. I have to breathe now. I can't run
35 without breathing. Half-blinded by my mask I trip and fall, crashing my head against the trench wall, knocking myself half-senseless. My gas mask has come off. I pull it down, but I have breathed in and know already it's too late.

feverishly in a state of intense excitement
firestep a step that ran along the length of a trench. It allowed soldiers to see over the top
no-man's-land the area of land between the two front lines
tendril a thin leaf or stem of a plant that twists around a support
dugout trench

Key Reading

Narrative texts

This is a **narrative** text. Its **purpose** is to tell a story in an entertaining way.

The main features of this text are:

● It has a **structure** that includes an opening (**introduction**), a problem (**complication**), a big moment when everything comes to a head (**crisis**) and an ending (**resolution**). For example, the introduction describes the scene before the gas attack.

● It has **characters**, who the story is about. We often hear their words and thoughts. In this text the **narrator** is one of the characters and tells the story in the first person, for example, '*I'm* shouting inside *my* gas mask'.

● It uses **expressive** and **descriptive** language, for example, 'Its *deadly tendrils* are searching ahead, feeling their way forward…'

1 What is the narrative **about**?

2 Where does the introduction to this episode **end**?

3 **a)** How much of this narrative is **description** and how much is **dialogue**?

  b) 'We fumble clumsily, feverishly with our gas masks.' Which words make this description **effective**?

4 Which **words** in the first two sentences show that it is a **first-person narrative**?

Purpose

5 What is the **main purpose** of this text?

- To write an account of an actual gas attack in the First World War.
- To tell the reader what gas attacks were like, but in an entertaining way as part of a story.
- To tell a story of how someone was the victim of a gas attack.
- To show how terrible war can be.

Point to evidence in the text to support your answer.

Reading for meaning

6 This narrative is written in the present tense.

a) Find two verbs in the present tense in the first paragraph.

b) Why do you think the writer has chosen the present tense? What does it bring to the story?

7 Who says "Gas! Gas!" (line 7)? Why doesn't the writer make it clear?

8 'Its deadly tendrils are searching ahead, feeling their way forward in long yellow wisps, scenting me, searching for me.' (lines 16–17).

a) The '-ing' form of the verb is used four times in this sentence. **Find two more sentences** where the '-ing' form is used a lot.

b) What **effect** do all these '-ing' verbs have?

9 The focus of the first half of this text is on the group of soldiers as a whole. In the second half the focus is on Private Peaceful.

a) Scan the text for the **first-person pronouns** 'we', 'us', 'I' and 'me'. What do you find?

b) Imagine you were directing a film of this book. How could the **camerawork** reflect this change in focus?

Focus on: Imagery

An image is a picture. **Imagery**, therefore, is simply the way in which writers help you picture what is going on. They do this by using words and ideas in an imaginative way, especially:

● by using powerful verbs, nouns, adjectives and adverbs

● by comparing things in an unusual way.

Look at this example from the extract:

powerful words

The gas is compared to a cloud. The word implies something dark and threatening

…we see it rolling towards us, this dreaded killer cloud…

10 In pairs, **draw up a table** to analyse how Michael Morpurgo has used imagery to describe the gas in lines 15–23.

● In column 1, copy out the **imagery** from the text.

● In column 2, list the **powerful words** used.

● In column 3, identify what the gas is being **compared** with, and comment on the **effect**.

You may want to begin your table like this:

Description of gas from text (imagery)	Powerful words and effect	Comparison and effect
'…we see it rolling towards us, this dreaded killer cloud…'	rolling – like something mechanical dreaded – like…	a cloud – something large and threatening
'Its deadly tendrils are searching ahead… searching for me'		

11 At times, the gas is described almost as a **person**.

a) **Find two examples** of this from your table.

b) Why is this idea particularly effective in a **war setting**?

Key Writing

Tanks were used for the first time in 1916, at the Battle of Flers. They were huge, lumbering machines, but they stunned the Germans.

12 You are **writing a story** from the point of view of a German soldier at the battle of Flers. You want to **describe his first sighting of the tank attack** in an effective way.

Wr5

a) Discuss with a partner what the picture of the tank below reminds you of. Can you use the comparisons you come up with as **images** in your description?

● Decide what the tanks are doing as they approach – how do they cope with the terrain? Are they firing at you?

● Brainstorm some powerful words to include in the description.

● Use the present tense to make the description more vivid.

b) Now **draft** a description of **six to eight sentences** on your own. You may want to begin like this:

We thought it was thunder at first. Hans and I looked at each other, then glanced at the sky. It was cloudless and bright.

c) Swap your description with a partner's. Give them **feedback** on how **effective** it is. Suggest ways in which the language and imagery could be improved. Then **redraft** your own description, taking on board your partner's comments.

② The silent ship

❱ Read an extract from a book about the *Mary Celeste* mystery

❱ Remind yourself of the key features of discursive texts

❱ Think about the effects of using different tenses (S4)

❱ Explore different ways of making your writing tentative (S5)

The following text is from a book for young people about the *Mary Celeste*.

The True Mystery of the *Mary Celeste*

Time: Afternoon of 4th December 1872.

Place: The Atlantic Ocean, between the Azores and the coast of Portugal.

Scene: A two-masted sailing ship is spotted by another ship,
5   drifting aimlessly. A small search party boards the ship.
         They find her to be well-stocked with food and fit to sail,
         but without a single soul on board.

● The name of this silent ship? The *Mary Celeste*.

● The cause of her passengers' and crew's disappearance?
10   Nobody knows.

Over the years, there have been shiploads of theories to explain
the disappearance of the *Mary Celeste*'s crew. Here are some of
the solutions that have taken the sea-sleuthing world by storm.

Were the missing crewmen kippered by a squid?

15 In 1904 a magazine article claimed that the entire ship's company
had been abducted by a giant octopus! According to the article,
the well-armed creature rose from the deep and grabbed the

ship's helmsman. The helmsman's yells brought the rest of the crew up on deck and, one by one, the octopus swept them up.

20 But could this have been what happened? Well, giant squid can be 20m (60ft) long, with eyes the size of a human head. But if a monster squid is the answer to the riddle, why did all hands remain on deck long enough to be plucked off in turn? And why did the squid make off with the ship's logbook, papers and lifeboat?

Did plundering pirates kill Captain Briggs and his crew?

25 Some people have suggested that pirates murdered Captain Briggs, his family and crew. But if pirates were to blame, where were the traces of violence you'd expect to see after a raid? And if sea-robbers had swarmed aboard the *Mary Celeste*, why hadn't they looted the ship

30 from stem to stern? Amongst the things found on board were a silver watch, a fancy sword, some gold jewellery and expensive clothes.

Were the crewmen scared witless (and shipless) by an iceberg?

35 It has been suggested that the crewmen abandoned ship to escape from an iceberg coming their way…although what an enormous chunk of ice was doing floating about the warm waters of the Azores is anyone's guess.

So what is the answer to this unfathomable mystery?

40 The maddening truth is, we shall probably never be able to prove any likely theory as to the *Mary Celeste*'s fate. The clues to its mystery, like its leading characters, are all long gone. Only the sea now knows what really happened on that fateful day in 1872… and

45 the sea keeps its secrets well.

Azores a group of islands	**hands** crew
aimlessly with no direction or aim	**logbook** sailing record
sleuth detective	**from stem to stern** from end to end
kippered finished off (in this sense)	**scared witless** scared out of their wits
abducted snatched, carried off	**unfathomable** impossible to solve

173

Key Reading

Discursive texts

This is a **discursive** text. Its **purpose** is to help someone understand an issue or debate by presenting the arguments fairly.

The main features of this text are:

- It has a form which consists of an **opening statement**, a series of different **points**, supported by **detail** or **evidence**, and a **conclusion**, for example, 'According to the article, the well-armed creature…' introduces a piece of detail.

- It has **phrases at the start of sentences** to signal which view you are writing about, for example, '*Some people* have suggested…'

- It uses **tentative language** to suggest different possibilities or ideas, for example, 'But if pirates were to blame, where were the traces of violence you'd expect to see after a raid?'

Grammar for reading

Tentative language is language which is cautious in its expression, for example: '*One answer might be…This could mean…*' This enables the writer to explore possibilities without stating an idea firmly.

1 What is the **issue** or **debate** in this discursive text? Which section tells you this?

2 **How many** different theories about the crew's disappearance are presented in this text?

3 What is the **main point** made about the first theory in lines 15–24? What **extra detail** is given to back up that point?

4 Which words in lines 26–31 suggest that the crewmen may **not** have been abducted by a giant squid?

5 Line 35 begins 'It has been suggested…'. What does this phrase tell you about the sentence that will **follow**?

• •

Purpose

6 What do you think is the **main purpose** of this text?

- To describe exactly what happened to the *Mary Celeste*.

- To present different people's theories about what happened, and assess these ideas.

- To dismiss everyone else's theories and come up with a new one.

- To present information about the *Mary Celeste* mystery in an entertaining way.

Point to evidence in the text to support your answer.

• •

Reading for meaning

7 How does the writer **introduce** this text (lines 1–13)? Discuss:

- the fact file **format** of the introduction

- the **tense** of the verbs

- how **effective** it is as an introduction to a mystery.

The present tense is often used in discursive texts to describe what people think now about an issue, for example, 'Here are some of the solutions that have taken the sea-sleuthing world by storm.' (lines 12–13). However, most of this text has verbs in the past tense.

S4

8 a) Identify three verbs in the **past tense**.

b) Explain why the author has used this tense.

9 Discursive texts often present several different theories. So it is important that the writing is well organised.
How does the author **organise** her text into sections to make it clear which theory is being discussed?

· ·

Focus on: The language of possibility

Discursive texts present different theories, views or explanations for something. The language is often **tentative**, as these are **possible** theories rather than facts. There are several ways in which possibility can be expressed:

● by the **verbs** that introduce the theories, for example, '*claimed* that'

● by using '**can**', '**could**' or '**may**' with a verb, for example, 'giant squid *can* be 20m long'

● by using an '**if**' clause, for example, '*if* a monster squid is the answer…'.

10 Reread lines 14–45 of the *Mary Celeste* text.

a) In pairs, note down one example of each type of **tentative language** listed above.

b) Rewrite one of these examples so that it becomes a **fact rather than a possibility**. Which words have you changed or removed? For example, *'It has been confirmed that the crewmen abandoned ship to escape an iceberg…'*

Key Writing

Here is another theory about what happened to the *Mary Celeste*.

> **Theory**: Captain Briggs went mad and murdered his family and crew before throwing himself into the sea.
>
> **For**: It must have been stressful being cooped up on a small ship. Such an event actually happened in 1828.
>
> **Against**: He was a very experienced captain. The ship's lifeboat and logbook were also missing.

Wr16 **11** Your task is to **write a paragraph** in the **same style** as the discursive text, putting forward both sides of this theory.

- Give your paragraph a heading in the form of a question.
- Introduce the theory at the beginning, using a phrase such as 'Another theory is', or 'Some people think'.
- Make your language tentative, for example, by using words like 'could' or 'would'. Try to include an 'if' clause.

177

 ③ Roman Wall Blues

 Aims

▸ Read a poem about a Roman soldier

▸ Remind yourself about the key features of poetry

▸ Practise using quotations from the poem to back up your points (Wr17)

▸ Prepare a presentation of the poem to give to the class (S&L3)

The following is a poem by W.H. Auden (1907–1973).

Roman Wall Blues

Over the heather the wet wind blows,
I've lice in my tunic and a cold in my nose.

The rain comes pattering out of the sky,
I'm a Wall soldier, I don't know why.

5 The mist creeps over the hard grey stone,
My girl's in Tungria; I sleep alone.

Aulus goes hanging around her place,
I don't like his manners, I don't like his face.

Piso's a Christian, he worships a fish;
10 There'd be no kissing if he had his wish.

She gave me a ring but I diced it away;
I want my girl and I want my pay.

When I'm a veteran with only one eye
I shall do nothing but look at the sky.

Wall Hadrian's Wall, a Roman
wall built across northern
England to keep out invaders
Tungria an Italian town
fish used as a symbol by early
Christians
diced gambled
veteran retired soldier

Key Reading

Poetry

This text is a **poem**. Its **purpose** is to explore feelings and ideas.

A poem is made up of **images**, **rhythm** and **form**.

- The **images** are the pictures made by the words, for example, 'The mist creeps over the hard grey stone.'

- The **form** is the framework or pattern of the poem. Poems are written in *lines*, not sentences, for example, the lines of this poem are grouped in twos.

- The **rhythm** is like the beat in music, for example, 'I've <u>lice</u> in my <u>tunic</u> and a <u>cold</u> in my <u>nose</u>…' (Underlined words show where the beat comes.)

Other important features of poetry are:

- Some poems **rhyme** and use other **sound effects**. This poem rhymes, for example: 'blows'/'nose', 'sky'/'why'.

- Some poems are **free verse.** They have lines of different lengths with different rhythms.

1 a) **Who** is this poem about?

b) **Where** and **when** is it set?

2 What **image** or picture do you get when you read the first three lines?

3 What do you notice about the **length of the sentences**? How do they fit the pattern of the poem?

4 Read the first few lines out loud. Where are the **main beats** (or stresses)? How many beats are there in each line? (See above for an example of where the beats come in line 2.)

5 There are lots of 'is' sounds in lines 9–10. What **effect** does this have? (Think carefully about the soldier's opinion of Piso.)

Purpose

6 What do you think is the **main purpose** of this poem?
- To give an unusual view of a famous historical period.
- To tell a story about a Roman soldier.
- To give facts about life in Roman Britain.
- To make you imagine what it was like to be a Roman soldier.

Give reasons for your choice.

Reading for meaning

7 a) The poem is written in the **first person** (i.e. from the point of view of the main character). What **effect** does this have?

b) Try rewriting a line or two as if it is about **someone else** (he, she, it) and then compare the two. For example:

> I've lice in my tunic and a cold in my nose.

> He had lice in his tunic and a cold in his nose.

8 a) Which lines describe the **setting** on Hadrian's Wall?

b) What kind of place is it?

c) What do you think the soldier feels about it?

9 The poem quickly moves its focus from the setting to the **thoughts** of the soldier himself. **Draw a spidergram** of all the thoughts and feelings that he has, like the one below.

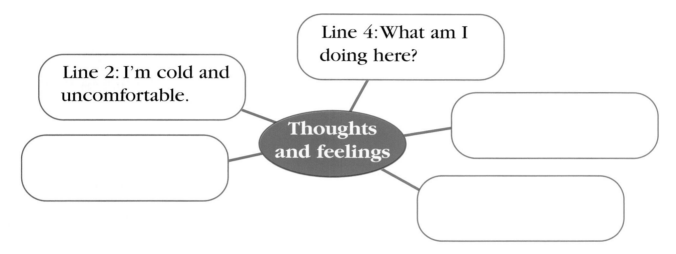

Line 4: What am I doing here?

Line 2: I'm cold and uncomfortable.

Thoughts and feelings

10 The poem is written in **rhyming couplets**, and has a strong sense of rhythm. Explore the **effect** of the rhyme. Which of these opinions do you agree with? Or do you have your own views?

Like most of the words – and the rhythm – the rhyme is simple and straightforward.

The rhymes are so obvious – almost childish – that it has a comic effect.

The rhyme is very predictable and plodding – like the rhythm. This is like the boredom of the soldier's life on the wall.

Grammar for reading

Rhyming couplets are a form of poetry in which lines are written in pairs. Each line in the pair ends with the same sound.

Focus on: Using quotations

When you write down or present your ideas about a poem (or any text, for that matter), it is important to support your points with evidence.

Follow these rules when you quote from a text:

- make your point first, then use a relevant quote to support it
- only quote short passages – a few words or lines at most
- try to work your quote into the sentence, rather than tag it on as an extra sentence.

Point made clearly at the beginning

The poem is full of the soldier's worries, which gives it an anxious tone overall. For example, the 'hard grey stone' of the wall makes the soldier think of how hard and grey it is away from his girlfriend. The couplet ends, 'I sleep alone'. 'Alone' sounds as miserable as its rhyme – 'the hard grey stone'.

Evidence is then given for the main point. This includes relevant quotations

- **Quotes** are worked into the sentence, not tagged on as separate sentences
- **Short quotations** are used
- Each quote begins and ends with an **inverted comma**

11 In pairs, you are going to write one or two sentences about the **sound effects** used in this poem.

Wr17

a) First of all, discuss what sound effects there are.

b) Then work out the one main point that you want to make.

c) Find one or two quotes that support your point. Finally, work the quotes into your sentence to provide the evidence.

Key Speaking and Listening

12 Work in pairs to **prepare a presentation** on *Roman Wall Blues*.
You will need to organise your thoughts about these aspects of
the poem:

- its subject
- its structure (how it is laid out)
- its use of rhythm
- its use of rhyme.

a) Each **make short notes** on two of these aspects, so that
together you cover all four. Try to make two or three main
points on each aspect and jot these down on a prompt card
like the one below.

> **Subject**
> - Roman soldier on sentry duty

b) Make sure you can **quote evidence** from the text when you
make your points. Add quotes to your card.

c) Finally, **practise your presentation**. Use your card as a
prompt – do not read from it directly.

d) Add a sentence or two at the end saying whether you like the
poem. Remember to give your reasons.

④ Unit 8 Assignment: The soldier poet

Assessment Focus

▶ **AF1** Write imaginative, interesting and thoughtful texts

> **You:** are a poet.
>
> **Your task:** to write a poem about an ordinary soldier in the Second World War.

Stage 1

Your poem will be about the D-Day invasions of France in the Second World War. However, it will look at this great event from your soldier's point of view.

Discuss with a partner **what you know** about the D-Day invasions. The facts below will start you off.

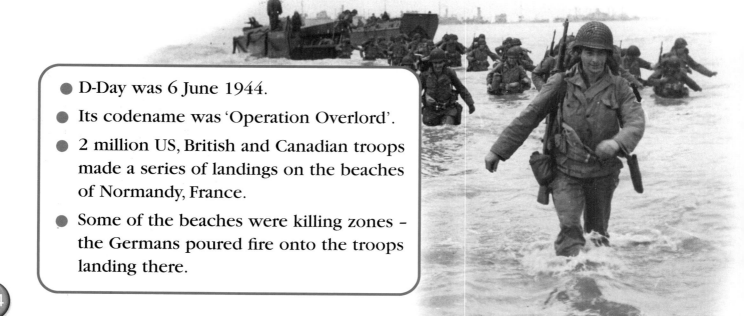

- D-Day was 6 June 1944.
- Its codename was 'Operation Overlord'.
- 2 million US, British and Canadian troops made a series of landings on the beaches of Normandy, France.
- Some of the beaches were killing zones – the Germans poured fire onto the troops landing there.

Stage 2

Now you need to get under the skin of your character. What might have been his concerns during (or before) this great event? **Brainstorm** his possible thoughts and feelings with your partner. You could record your ideas in a spidergram like this:

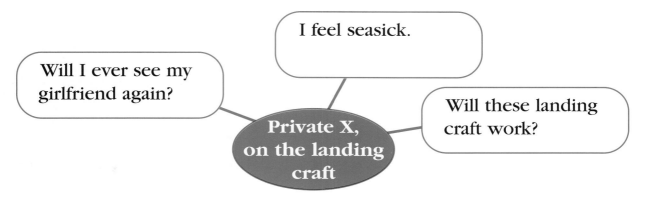

Stage 3

Using these ideas, **draft your own poem**. Follow these tips:

● Your poem should be written in couplets. Aim to write only three or four couplets.

● Give it a strong rhythm and rhyme.

● Focus on the private thoughts and feelings of your character.

● Don't explain in the poem what historical event the soldier is part of. This will be done by your poem's title. So think carefully what you will call your poem.

Challenge

Can you use **sound effects** in your poem?

Apart from using sound effects in rhyme, you could also include words beginning with the same letter or letters (for example, shrieking shells). This is called **alliteration**.

① Hey dude – what's an extreme sport?

Aims

▷ Read an information text from a website

▷ Explore degrees of formality in texts (S12)

▷ Look at how a text changes when it is made more formal (S10)

▷ Adapt a short information text

The following text comes from a website for young people called *The Site*.

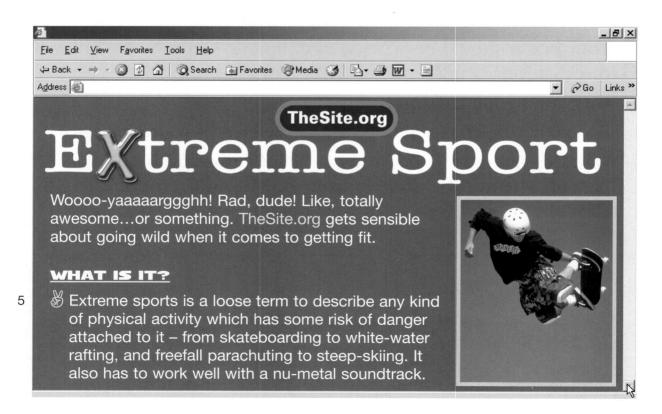

TheSite.org

Extreme Sport

Woooo-yaaaaarggghh! Rad, dude! Like, totally awesome…or something. TheSite.org gets sensible about going wild when it comes to getting fit.

WHAT IS IT?

5 ✌ Extreme sports is a loose term to describe any kind of physical activity which has some risk of danger attached to it – from skateboarding to white-water rafting, and freefall parachuting to steep-skiing. It also has to work well with a nu-metal soundtrack.

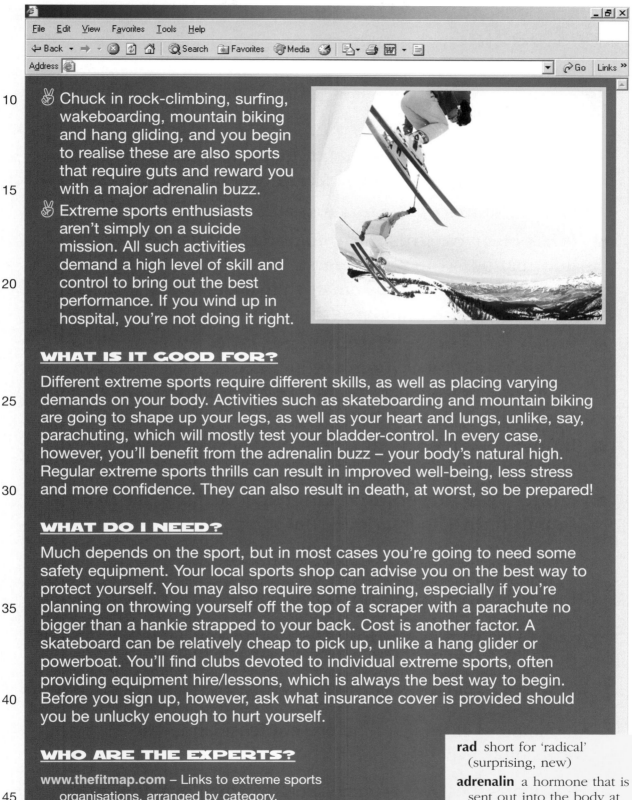

10 ✌ Chuck in rock-climbing, surfing, wakeboarding, mountain biking and hang gliding, and you begin to realise these are also sports that require guts and reward you
15 with a major adrenalin buzz.

✌ Extreme sports enthusiasts aren't simply on a suicide mission. All such activities demand a high level of skill and
20 control to bring out the best performance. If you wind up in hospital, you're not doing it right.

WHAT IS IT GOOD FOR?

Different extreme sports require different skills, as well as placing varying
25 demands on your body. Activities such as skateboarding and mountain biking are going to shape up your legs, as well as your heart and lungs, unlike, say, parachuting, which will mostly test your bladder-control. In every case, however, you'll benefit from the adrenalin buzz – your body's natural high. Regular extreme sports thrills can result in improved well-being, less stress
30 and more confidence. They can also result in death, at worst, so be prepared!

WHAT DO I NEED?

Much depends on the sport, but in most cases you're going to need some safety equipment. Your local sports shop can advise you on the best way to protect yourself. You may also require some training, especially if you're
35 planning on throwing yourself off the top of a scraper with a parachute no bigger than a hankie strapped to your back. Cost is another factor. A skateboard can be relatively cheap to pick up, unlike a hang glider or powerboat. You'll find clubs devoted to individual extreme sports, often providing equipment hire/lessons, which is always the best way to begin.
40 Before you sign up, however, ask what insurance cover is provided should you be unlucky enough to hurt yourself.

WHO ARE THE EXPERTS?

www.thefitmap.com – Links to extreme sports
45 organisations, arranged by category.

www.skateparkpages.co.uk – Find a skate park near you, for skateboarding or BMX.

www.britsurf.co.uk – Surf's up, and this site will sort you out with decent waves, coaching, gear, etc.

rad short for 'radical' (surprising, new)

adrenalin a hormone that is sent out into the body at times of stress or danger

enthusiast someone who loves what they do

Key Reading

Information texts

This text is an **information** text. Its **purpose** is to present information on a subject in a clear and/or interesting way.

The main features of this text text are:

- It has **clear organisation**. Important or general information is often given first. The information is arranged in paragraphs or separate sections, for example, 'Extreme sports is a loose term to…'

- It uses verbs in the **present** tense, for example, '…these are also sports that *require* guts'. This text also uses verbs in other tenses, such as the **future**, for example, '…in every case you *will benefit* from…'

- It often uses **technical terms** or specialist words, for example, 'steep-skiing'.

- It often uses **impersonal language**, i.e. language that sounds formal and 'serious'. But this text also uses quite personal and informal language, for example:
  Formal: 'Cost is another factor'
  Informal: 'If you wind up in hospital'.

1 What is the **subject** of this information text?

2 Find another example of the **present tense** under the subheading 'What do I need?'.

3 **How many** specialist extreme sports are mentioned? List them.

4 Can you find a chatty, or **informal word or phrase** used in the very first line of the article?

Purpose

The main purpose of the text is to gives readers a basic introduction to extreme sports. But what else does it do?

5 Read the table below, which shows three possible additional purposes of the *Extreme Sport* text. Check the text for any evidence of these purposes. Then copy and **complete the table** below, with the evidence you find.

Purpose	Yes – give evidence	No
To entertain us – make us laugh		
To warn of the dangers of some extreme sports	*'ask what insurance cover is provided'* *(last section)*	
To encourage the reader to find out more		

Reading for meaning

The text is divided into main sections with different headings:

● What is it?

● What is it good for?

● What do I need?

6 a) Which section deals mainly with **equipment and clubs**?

b) Which section deals mainly with what extreme sports **are**?

c) Which section deals mainly with how extreme sports will **help our bodies**?

7 The article tells us about how you might feel while doing extreme sports. What do you think the writer means when she says you can get an 'adrenalin buzz'? **Write a sentence** to explain what you think.

· ·

Focus on: Informal and formal texts

Sometimes we can write or speak in an **informal** way:

> Oi! Wait up. I'm gonna be there in a mo.

Sometimes, it is better to use a more **formal** style:

> Excuse me. Can you wait, please, sir? I will be there in a moment.

In the information text about extreme sports, the writer wants to make the information *clear*, so some things are quite formal. But she is also writing for young people, about young people's sports. So, she sometimes writes **informally**, and speaks **directly to the reader** (that is, you).

S10 **8** One section below has been rewritten in formal language from informal language.

a) First, decide which is the original, **informal** version.

b) Then, identify **what has been changed** in the other text. Try to be as precise as possible.

A Chuck in rock-climbing, surfing, wakeboarding, mountain biking and hang gliding, and you begin to realise these are also sports that require guts…

B Include rock-climbing, surfing, wakeboarding, mountain biking and hang gliding, and one realises that these are also sports that require bravery…

9 Here are some other informal words or phrases from the text. Write down the more **formal alternatives**:

- *totally awesome!*
- a major *buzz*
- if you *wind up* in hospital
- *hankie.*

Key Writing

S12 **10** Your task is to help make this text, written for young climbers, **more suitable for older people.**

a) Read it first. The informal sections have been highlighted.

> Climbing is a well-cool thing to do. When I'm perched on top of some peak, I feel like a million dollars, but you don't get there by luck.
>
> You gotta get real. If you wanna get a buzz out of it, you need to do it safely.
>
> You'll need the proper stuff – and the right guys around you. It's no use being surrounded by your mates who have never seen a mountain in their lives.
>
> Nah. I reckon you need expert help. Dudes who know what they're blabbin' on about.

b) Now, **rewrite it**, using some of the words and phrases given below. Be careful – not all of them work.

fantastic	so proud	must understand	must face the facts
want to	have to	thrill	equipment
singing about	good feeling	clothes	toys
people	wonderful	brilliant	no
not	not at all	friends	talking about
food	believe	feel	think

② How to do a bungee-jump

Aims

▶ Read an explanation text (which also uses instructions)

▶ Revise and develop your skills as a critical reader (R4)

▶ Perform a commentary (S&L4)

The following text comes from a science website, but it is about bungee-jumping – the sport where people leap from bridges, buildings or aircraft, attached to a long elastic lead.

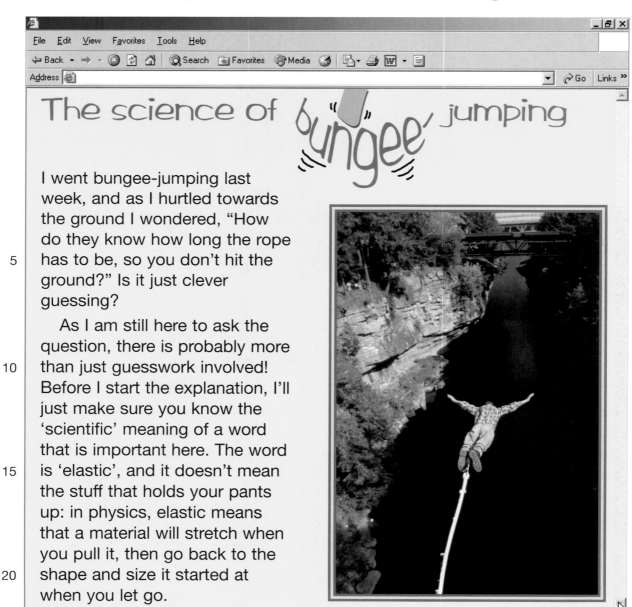

The science of bungee jumping

I went bungee-jumping last week, and as I hurtled towards the ground I wondered, "How do they know how long the rope
5   has to be, so you don't hit the ground?" Is it just clever guessing?

   As I am still here to ask the question, there is probably more
10   than just guesswork involved! Before I start the explanation, I'll just make sure you know the 'scientific' meaning of a word that is important here. The word
15   is 'elastic', and it doesn't mean the stuff that holds your pants up: in physics, elastic means that a material will stretch when you pull it, then go back to the
20   shape and size it started at when you let go.

File Edit View Favorites Tools Help

⇐ Back ▼ → ▼ ⊗ ⊡ ⌂ | ⊗Search ⌐Favorites ⌐Media ⊘ | ⊡▼ ⊟ ⊎ ▼ ⊟

Address ⬒

Now, let's do a bungee-jump in miniature. Get a long, thin elastic rubber band, and hang it from a hook or a door handle; that's the bungee rope. Next, put a weight on the bottom end of the band – a lump of plasticine will do; that's you. (I know you don't look like a lump of plasticine, but this is just an experiment, so either use your imagination or your artistic talent to sort it out.) What's happened? Correct! The rubber band has stretched. It is now longer than when we started, because the force (weight) of the plasticine is pulling down on the end. However, that's you at the end of the jump. What about the "Jump off the bridge and shout 'Neeeyaaargh!'" part at the start?

If you lift the plasticine and then drop it, you will see it goes lower because the band stretches more, then it gets shorter and jerks the plasticine up again. The elastic rope does the same to you, and you bounce up and down a few times before you stop.

If you do the same thing again, the plasticine will go down the same distance each time before it is pulled up. This happens because the rubber band stretches more for a big force than it does for a small force, but it always stretches the same amount with the same force.

When you jump off a bridge on a bungee-rope, the experts have worked out, with some clever maths, exactly how much your weight will stretch the rope as you fall. (This is something you can do with elastic materials, using a discovery made by Robert Hooke.) They can measure just the right length to make sure that you get very close to the river, ground or whatever is under the bridge, but you don't actually hit it. Of course, bungee-jumpers should never lie about their weight!

Key Reading

Explanation texts

This text is mainly an **explanation** text. Its **purpose** is to explain how something happens in a clear way. However, in order to do this it also includes **instructions**.

The main features of this text are:

- It has a series of **clear and logical steps**, for example, the first and second paragraph of the main text (lines 1–21) make it clear exactly what this text is setting out to explain.

- It uses **causal language** which shows how one thing causes another, for example:

effect   cause

you will see it goes lower because the band stretches more

- It uses **formal** and **impersonal language**, often including **technical** and **specialist** words and phrases, for example, 'It is now longer than when we started, because the *force* (weight) of the plasticine is pulling down on the end'.

- It has verbs in the **present tense**, to make general points or explain rules, for example, 'it always *stretches* the same amount with the same force'

- It sometimes uses **other tenses** too – perhaps to explain an effect. For example, 'What's *happened*? Correct! The rubber band *has stretched*'.

1 The writer uses an experiment to explain how a bungee jump works.

   a) What are the main **materials** in the experiment?

   b) What do they **replace** from the 'real' jump?

2 Can you find a sentence in paragraph 5 that describes *why* something happens (i.e. **the cause**)?

3 Find an example of the **present tense** in paragraph 3.

• •

Purpose

The main purpose of this text is to explain *how* and *why* something happens. But there are also moments when the writer *instructs* the reader.

4 What does the writer give **instructions** about?

5 We can tell the writer is also using instructions from the sorts of words and phrases he uses. For example, he uses **imperative verbs**.

   a) Find at least **two examples** of these sorts of verbs from paragraph 3.

   The writer also uses **time** and **sequence connectives**, such as 'Now', which starts paragraph 3.

   b) Write down the other time connective in the same paragraph.

Grammar for reading

Imperative verbs tell (or **command**) you directly to do something, for example, *'Take a long piece of tubing…'*

Time and **sequence connectives** show the order in which things must be done, for example, *'Next take a long piece of tubing…'*

6 This text comes from a science website, which is really showing what 'elastic' and 'force' mean. But how does the writer stop this from becoming boring? In pairs, **find examples** of the writer doing each of the following:

- telling the reader about something he did **in his own life**
- mentioning another type of elastic that readers might find **funny**
- asking the reader **direct questions**, as if he's talking to them.

Reading for meaning

7 At the end of the text the writer mentions some 'clever maths' and a 'discovery' by Robert Hooke. Why doesn't he explain this maths and this discovery in any detail? Think carefully about the **audience** (the readers) and the **purpose** of the text.

8 Many explanation texts also include design features such as:

- bullet points
- subheadings
- images or diagrams
- numbering.

a) Look back at the text and note down **two ways** you could **improve the layout**.

b) **Explain** at least one of these changes, for example:

Add a subheading above paragraph 3 instead of the first sentence, like this.

Mini bungee jump

Get a long, thin elastic rubber band, and hang it from a hook or a door handle...

Focus on: Writing your own explanation or commentary

As you have seen, good explanations are able to make processes clear. Part of the way this is done is by showing *cause and effect*. Read this voice-over for a science television programme:

Lions *spend* much of the day asleep, *in order to* conserve energy.

cause

effect

During such programmes the experts often speak using the present tense, describing and explaining what they see.

Here we are, driving through the African bush, *looking* for a pride of lions.

9 Try **linking these short sentences** together, choosing from the connectives listed below to bring out the cause and effect.

- as
- so that
- in order to
- as a result

a) We are camping near the caves. We can see the bats at night-time.

b) I am standing near the edge of the cliff face. I can just see the chicks emerging from the nest.

c) We are travelling a long distance today. We need to be on the river early next morning.

Key Speaking and Listening

10 The four images below show somebody doing a skateboard trick – 'the Acid Drop' or 'Drop off'. You are going to **explain to a friend how to do it**. Use the captions to help you.

This is perfect.

1 The right place.

2 Both feet on board.

3 Using the tail.

4 Moving feet into position.

For example:

> Picture 1: Here I am doing the Acid Drop. It's best to find a drop followed by a flat surface when you start, because if it's too steep, it's difficult to control your board.
>
> Picture 2: Now, here I am...

Remember to:

● use the **present tense**

● use **connectives** to show cause and effect

● include some **informal language** to make it interesting for your audience.

Touching the void

Aims

▶ Read an exciting, real-life account to do with climbing

▶ Explore different types of sentences and their effects on the reader (S2)

▶ Write your own recount text

The following text is from a book by Joe Simpson about two men who are on a climbing trip that goes terribly wrong. In this section, Simon is wondering what has happened to his companion, Joe, who has fallen down the ice. He can't see him but can feel him at the end of the rope below.

As the rope ran out I realised that the pressure wasn't easing. Joe was still hanging free. What in hell's name was I lowering him over?

I looked down at the slack rope being fed through the belay plate. Twenty feet below I spotted the knot coming steadily towards me. I began swearing,
5   trying to urge Joe to touch down on to something solid. At ten feet I stopped lowering. The pressure on the rope hadn't changed.

I kept stamping my feet. I was trying to halt the collapse of the seat but it wasn't working. I felt the first shivers of fear. Snow hit me again from behind, surging over and around me. My thighs moved down fractionally.
10 The avalanche pushed me forward and filled the seat behind my back. Oh God! I'm coming off.

Then it stopped as abruptly as it had started. I let the rope slide five feet, thinking
15 furiously. Could I hold the rope with one hand below the knot and change the plate over? I lifted one hand from the rope and stared at it. I couldn't
20 squeeze it into a fist. I thought of holding the rope locked against the plate by winding it round my thigh and then releasing the plate from my
25 harness. Stupid idea! I couldn't hold Joe's weight with my hands

alone. If I released the plate, 150 feet of free rope would run unstoppably through my hands, and then it would rip me clear off the mountain.

30　It had been nearly an hour since Joe had gone over the drop. I was shaking with cold. My grip on the rope kept easing despite my efforts. The rope slowly edged down and the knot pressed against my right fist. I can't hold it, can't stop it. The thought overwhelmed me. The snow slides and wind and cold were forgotten. I was being pulled off. The seat moved beneath me, and snow slipped away past my feet. I slipped a few inches. Stamping my feet deep into
35　the slope halted the movement. God! I had to do something!

The knife! The thought came out of nowhere. Of course, the knife. Be quick, come on, get it.

The knife was in my sack. It took an age to let go a hand and slip the strap off my shoulder, and then repeat it with the other hand. I braced the rope
40　across my thigh and held on to the plate with my right hand as hard as I could. Fumbling at the catches on the rucksack, I could feel the snow slowly giving way beneath me. Panic threatened to swamp me. I felt in the sack, searching desperately for the knife. My hand closed round something smooth and I pulled it out. The red plastic handle slipped in my mitt and I nearly dropped it.
45　I put it in my lap before tugging my mitt off with my teeth. I had already made the decision. There was no other option left to me. The metal blade stuck to my lips when I opened it with my teeth.

I reached down to the rope and then stopped. The slack rope! Clear the loose rope twisted round my foot! If it tangled it would rip me down with it. I
50　carefully cleared it to one side, and checked that it all lay in the seat away from the belay plate. I reached down again, and this time I touched the blade to the rope.

It needed no pressure. The taut rope exploded at the touch of the blade, and I flew backwards into the seat as the pulling strain vanished. I was shaking.
55　Leaning back against the snow, I listened to a furious hammering in my temple as I tried to calm my breathing. Snow hissed over me in a torrent. I ignored it as it poured over my face and chest, spurting into the open zip at my neck, and on down below. It kept coming. Washing across me and down after the cut rope, and after Joe.
60　I was alive, and for the moment that was all I could think about. Where Joe was, or whether he was alive, didn't concern me in the long silence after the cutting. His weight had gone from me. There was only the wind and the avalanches left to me.

When at last I sat up, the slack rope fell from my hips. One frayed end
65　protruded from the belay plate – he had gone. Had I killed him? I didn't answer the thought, though some urging in the back of my mind told me that I had. I felt numb. Freezing cold, and shocked into a numb silence, I stared bleakly into the swirling snow beneath me wondering at what had happened. There was no guilt, not even sorrow. I stared at the faint torch beam cutting
70　through the snow and felt haunted by its emptiness.

belay plate a piece of equipment that stops a climber falling
protruded stuck out

Key Reading

Recount texts

This text is a **recount**. Its **purpose** is to tell the reader about a series of real events, so that they can understand what happened.

The main features of this text are:

- It uses verbs in the **past tense**, for example, 'I *yelled*'.

- It features events in **time order** (chronological order), for example, '*It had been nearly an hour* since Joe had gone over the drop. I was shaking with cold.'

- It uses **time connectives**, for example, 'When *at last I* sat up, the slack rope fell from my hips.'

- The **paragraphs** generally show a **change in focus**, for example, one paragraph ends, 'I had to do something!'. The next paragraph begins, 'The knife! The thought came out of nowhere…'

- It uses **powerful descriptive language**, for example:

  adjective: '*shocked into a numb silence*'
  adverb: '*My thighs moved down fractionally*'
  verb: '*The thought overwhelmed me*'

1 The text concerns two men. Which one is **recounting** what happened?

2 This isn't just a text about what happened. It is also about the writer's feelings and emotions. Look for an example which tells us **how the writer feels** in paragraph 7.

3 In paragraph 4, one **time connective** is used twice to help the reader understand when things are happening. Can you identify this connective?

4 Can you find one example of an **adverb** in paragraph 4?

> **Grammar for reading**
>
> **Adverbs** tell us how something happened and add more information to verbs, for example, 'He walked quickly'.
>
> Adverbs usually end in 'ly' but not always, for example, 'The climb went well'.

Purpose

The writer clearly wants to tell us what happened. So to gain our interest and keep it, he describes:

● the **drama and tension** of what happened

● the **emotions** going through his mind

● the **exact events** in detail so that the key moment in the text **makes sense**, looking back.

5 Which of the following do you think is his **main purpose**?

● to describe what it's like climbing on an icy mountain

● to explain what led up to him cutting the rope

● to tell us how difficult mountaineering is.

Give reasons for your choice.

••••••••••••••••••••••••••••••

Reading for meaning

The text is full of descriptions of the conditions, and the writer's state of mind.

6 **Link descriptions** A–D with the **states of mind** (1–4).

1 feeling foolish

A I had to do something!

2 not concerned

B I was alive, and for the moment that was all I could think about.

C Snow hissed over me in a torrent. I ignored it as it poured over my face and chest….

3 feeling desperate, in a panic

D Stupid idea! I couldn't hold Joe's weight with my hands alone.

4 feeling relieved

••••••••••••••••••••••••••••••

Focus on: Different sentence structures

The writer uses many different types of sentence. This is to get across what happens and how he feels.

Here is one example:

The knife! The thought came out of nowhere. Of course, the knife. Be quick, come on, get it.

This series of short sentences shows how the thought about the knife suddenly appears in the writer's mind. It could have been written like this:

> Suddenly, I had a good idea which was that I could use the knife, so I decided to get it.

S2 **7** Why is the first version better than the second? (Think about the **mood** created and the **pace** of events.)

Sometimes a longer sentence is more suitable to explain in detail what happened.

> I felt in the sack, searching desperately for the knife.

This sentence is made up of two **clauses**. The first is the **main clause** describing the main action. This clause is complete and could be a sentence on its own.

> **I felt in the sack**, <u>searching</u> desperately for the knife.

The second is a **non-finite clause**. It comes after the comma and could not be a sentence on its own. The use of the continuous present verb 'searching' is very important because it describes what the writer is doing while he feels in the sack.

Usually, these sorts of sentences can be swapped around.

> <u>**Searching** desperately **for the knife**</u>, I felt in the sack.

S1 **8** Identify the **non-finite clause** in the sentence below. Remember, it does not make sense on its own. Also think about where the comma is.

> Fumbling at the catches on the rucksack, I could feel the snow slowly giving way beneath me.

Key Writing

9 You are now going to **write three descriptive sentences** of your own. Imagine you are Joe – at the bottom of the rope. Suddenly, you realise it has been cut!

a) Describe what happens next. In each case you will need to finish the sentence by adding a clause – either a **main clause** (could make a sentence on its own) or a **non-finite clause**.

- Hanging onto the rope, I suddenly _____.

  Add a simple verb and more detail

- I plunged through the air, _____.

  Add a continuous verb ending in '…ing' and more detail

- Reaching out for something to hold, I could feel _____.

  Add more detail to complete the sentence

b) Try writing two more sentences with two clauses about what happens to Joe. Then use all five sentences in a paragraph to complete the episode.

④ Unit 9 Assignment: Explorer

Assessment Focus

▶ AF4 Construct paragraphs and use cohesion within and between paragraphs

You: are an explorer back from a dangerous expedition. You have been tracing Captain Scott's last journey back from the South Pole with one other person, Sam Brooker.

Your task: to write an account of a particularly dangerous moment from your journey. It will form part of a chapter from a book you are writing.

Stage 1

Notes

Day 24 – Blizzard.
On the Beardmore Glacier
Heading for the Ross Sea
Temperature – 2 degrees Celsius
Sam has fever, can't go on
We pitch camp, and I call for assistance
Weather so bad helicopter cannot find
 us or land
We decide to try to get out of glacier before
 temperature drops any more
I pull Sam on a sled behind me
He's looking bad
Stop and check satellite navigation system
Isn't working. Can't go on
Suddenly helicopter appears out of nowhere
 and lands. Saved!

Stage 2

Plan paragraph 1. Decide what it's going to be about, for example:

> Date and location. Me walking through the snow; Sam behind me then falling to the ground...

Plan paragraphs 2 and 3 in the same way.

If it helps, use a timeline, like the one below to organise your notes. Then decide where the paragraph breaks will come and mark them as zigzags across the timeline.

Me walking
in snow, Sam
falling to ground

Stage 3

Now draft your three paragraphs.

Remember to:
- use the past tense (not the present tense of the notes)
- start it with a verb ending in 'ing', for example:
  'Staggering through the snow, I turned...'
- try to add at least one short sentence, for example:
  'Then I saw him. Sam! On the frozen ground...'
- include time connectives to make it clear to the reader what is happening when, for example: *'then'*, *'next'*, *'afterwards'*.

William Collins' dream of knowledge for all began with the publication of his first book in 1819. A self-educated mill worker, he not only enriched millions of lives, but also founded a flourishing publishing house. Today, staying true to this spirit, Collins books are packed with inspiration, innovation and practical expertise. They place you at the centre of a world of possibility and give you exactly what you need to explore it.

Collins. Do more.

Published by Collins
An imprint of HarperCollinsPublishers
77–85 Fulham Palace Road
Hammersmith
London
W6 8JB

Browse the complete Collins catalogue at
www.collinseducation.com

10 9 8 7 6 5 4 3 2 1

ISBN 0 00 719435 8

Mike Gould, Mary Green, John Mannion and Kim Richardson assert their moral rights to be identified as the authors of this work

British Library Cataloguing in Publication Data
A Catalogue record for this publication is available from the British Library

Acknowledgements
The following permissions to reproduce material are gratefully acknowledged:

Text: Extract from 'Dracula' by Bram Stoker, pp4–5; 'Alternative Endings to an Unwritten Ballad' by Paul Dehn, © The Estate of Max Beerbohm, reprinted by permission of Berlin Associates, pp11–12; extract from 'The Pig Scrolls' by Paul Shipton, (Puffin Books 2004) © Paul Shipton 2004, pp26–27; extract from '10 urban myths to chill you to the bone' from ivillage.co.uk, p33; extract from 'How Urban Legends Work' by Tom Harris from howstuffworks.com, pp33–34; extract from 'Robin Hood: Prince of thieves or just a petty thief?', from The National Museum of Australia website at nma.gov.org, pp40–41; extract from 'The Hook' by Kevin Crossley-Holland, OUP 1998, p47; extract from 'The Lord of the Rings' by J. R. R. Tolkien , reprinted by permission of HarperCollins Publishers Ltd © Tolkien 1954, pp50–51; 'The Nose' by Iain Crichton-Smith, from 'In the Middle' (Victor Gollancz Ltd 1977), pp58–59; Derren Brown's Tricks of the Mind, an Objective Productions production for Channel 4. Extract from Channel4.com courtesy of Channel 4 Television, pp65–66; extract from 'Hurricanes and Tornadoes' by Neil Morris (Ticktock Media 1999), pp74–75; extract from 'Tea Pests' (William Blackwood and Sons Ltd) by J. W. Beagle Atkins pp80–81; extract from 'The Birds' by Daphne du Maurier, taken from 'The Birds and Other Stories' (Penguin,1968), pp86–87; extract from 'Billy Elliot' by Lee Hall (Faber and Faber 2000) pp96–97; 'Writing for the Simpsons', from tinyonline.co.uk, pp102–103; extract from 'My Family brings humour to Christmas Day' from tvtoday.co.uk, pp108–109; extract from 'Refugee Boy' by Benjamin Zephaniah (Bloomsbury 2001), with permission from Bloomsbury Publishing, pp118–119; 'Refugees and Asylum Seekers – the Facts' from the Council for Racial Equality website at cre.gov.uk, pp125–126; STAR campaign leaflet reproduced with permission, pp131–132; extract from 'The Birth of The Bug' reproduced with permission of Pure Digital, pp142–143; extract from 'Don't believe the hype' by John O'Farrell, The Independent Newspaper, 17th February 2000, pp149–150; extract from 'So annoying, but they bring in the money' by Gina Davidson, reproduced with permission from The Scotsman Publications Limited, pp156–157; extract from 'Private Peaceful' by Michael Morpurgo, reprinted by permission of HarperCollins Publishers Ltd © Michael Morpurgo 2003, reproduced with permission from HarperCollins Publishers pp166–167; extract from 'The True History of the Mary Celeste' by Rachel Wright (Scholastic, 2001), reproduced with permission from Scholastic Ltd, pp172–173; 'Roman Wall Blues' from 'Collected Poems' by W. H. Auden (Faber and Faber) reproduced with permission from Faber and Faber, p178; 'Extreme Sport', reproduced with permission from thesite.org, pp186–187; 'The science of bungee jumping', from sciencenet.org.uk, pp192–193; extract from TOUCHING THE VOID by Joe Simpson published by Jonathon Cape. Used by permission of the Random House Group Limited, pp199–200.

Images: Alasdair Bright, NB Illustration: pp7, 9, 14, 15, 48, 180, 183, 198; Andy Ward, NB Illustration: pp58, 63; Aquarius Collection: pp21, 53, 56, 96, 99, 101, 102, 106, 107, 115; BBC: pp108, 112, 113; Corbis: pp186, 187, 190, 192, 193; Getty Images: pp25, 33, 74, 77, 79, 86, 88, 90, 95, 149, 153, 155, 159, 164; Marco Schaaf, NB Illustration: p72; Mary Evans Picture Library: pp17, 41, 45, 167, 173, 176; Matt Carr: p65; Movie Store Collection Ltd: pp22, 26, 43; PA Photos: pp80, Popperfoto: pp171, 184; Sarah Naylor, NB Illustration: pp30, 32.

Whilst every effort has been made both to contact the copyright holders and to give exact credit lines, this has not proved possible in every case.

Printed and bound by Printing Express, Hong Kong